A Guide To Eating After Gallbladder Surgery

Affan .W Curran

Introduction

This book serves as an essential guide for individuals managing their health and diet after gallbladder removal or for those dealing with gallstones.

The book begins with a comprehensive overview of gallstones, detailing signs, symptoms, and conditions under which they may be asymptomatic. It delves into the causes of gallstone formation, such as excessive cholesterol or bilirubin in the bile, and the impact of concentrated bile due to a full gallbladder.

Treatment options are thoroughly explored, including surgical methods like cholecystectomy, which is presented in two different forms, and nonsurgical therapies. The book also examines risk factors associated with gallstones, highlighting both lifestyle factors and medical conditions that may increase susceptibility.

An important segment of the book is dedicated to dietary management and foods beneficial for those without a gallbladder or with gallstones. It emphasizes the role of diet in prevention and offers detailed guidelines for maintaining a healthy gallbladder. The dietary recommendations include a variety of foods to incorporate, such as plant-based foods, lean proteins, and fiber-rich options. Specific nutrients like coffee, calcium, folate, magnesium, and vitamin C are also suggested for their beneficial effects.

Conversely, the book outlines foods to avoid, including refined carbohydrates and unhealthy fats, providing insights into specific food items that fall under these categories. Special attention is given to dietary adjustments post-gallbladder removal, advising avoidance of spicy and fatty foods to prevent discomfort and promote digestion.

The cookbook section presents a collection of simple and delicious recipes tailored for those without a gallbladder or managing gallstones. These recipes are designed to be gentle on the digestive system while being nutritious and satisfying.

This cookbook is an invaluable resource for anyone looking to navigate their dietary needs in the absence of a gallbladder or when dealing with gallstones. It combines medical insights with practical dietary advice, ensuring readers are well-equipped to make informed decisions about their health and diet.

Contents

CHAPTER 1 GUIDE TO GALLSTONES

The gallbladder is a pouch holding bile, a green-yellow liquid that aids digestion. Gallbladder problems often occur when something like a gallstone blocks the bile duct.

Most gallstones are created when substances found in bile, like cholesterol, harden.

Gallstones are very common and routinely asymptomatic. However, approximately 10% of patients diagnosed with gallstones will have symptoms within five years.

Gallstone signs and symptoms

Gallstones might cause pain in your upper right abdomen or stomach area. Gallbladder discomfort may occasionally occur after eating high-fat foods, such as fried dishes, but it can happen anytime. Gallstone pain typically lasts only a few hours, although it can be excruciating.

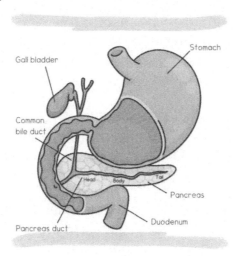

If gallstones are not treated or discovered, the following symptoms may develop:

- a fast heartbeat caused by a high temperature

- skin yellowing and whites of the eyes (jaundice)

- diarrhea, cold, and confusion

- a decrease in appetite

- Gallbladder infection or inflammation of the liver or pancreas can cause these symptoms.

Gallstones with no symptoms

Gallstones do not produce pain on their own. Pain develops when gallstones obstruct bile movement from the gallbladder.

According to the American College of Gastroenterology, "silent gallstones" affect approximately 80% of persons with gallstones. This indicates they are free of discomfort and symptoms. In these circumstances, your doctor may uncover gallstones via X-rays or during abdominal surgery.

Causes

Gallstones are thought to be caused by a chemical imbalance of bile within the gallbladder. While experts are yet unsure what causes the imbalance, there are a few probable explanations:

There is too much cholesterol.

A buildup of cholesterol in your bile might result in yellow cholesterol stones. Hard stones can form if your liver produces more cholesterol than your bile can break down.

There is much bilirubin in your bile.

Bilirubin is a substance created naturally during the breakdown of red blood cells. It is produced, passed via the liver, and subsequently eliminated from the body.

Some medical diseases, such as liver damage and blood disorders, lead your liver to produce more bilirubin than it should. When the gallbladder cannot break down excess bilirubin, pigment gallstones form. These rough stones are frequently dark brown or black.

Bile that has been concentrated due to a full gallbladder

To function effectively, your gallbladder must be able to empty its bile. If it does not open its bile content, the bitterness gets too concentrated, which can lead to the formation of stones.

Treatment

Most of the time, you won't need gallstone therapy until they cause you discomfort. Gallstones can travel through your body without your knowledge. If you are in agony, your doctor will most likely advise you to get surgery. Medication may be utilized in rare circumstances.

If you are at high risk of surgical complications, there are a few nonsurgical options for treating gallstones. However, your gallstones may return with continued treatment if surgery is not performed, implying you may need to monitor your condition for the rest of your life.

Surgery

Cholecystectomy, or gallbladder surgery, is one of the most common operations performed on adults in the United States. Because the gallbladder isn't a vital organ, you can live a healthy life without it.

Cholecystectomy comes in two varieties:

Cholecystectomy is performed laparoscopically. This is a standard procedure that necessitates general anesthesia. In most cases, the surgeon will make three or four incisions in your belly. They'll delicately remove your gallbladder after inserting a small, illuminated gadget into one of the incisions. If there are no issues, you can generally go home the same day or the next day.

Cholecystectomy with an open incision. This procedure is usually performed when the gallbladder is inflamed, diseased, or scarred. This operation may also be performed if complications arise during laparoscopic cholecystectomy.

Stools may be loose or watery after gallbladder ectomy. When a gallbladder is removed, the bile must be redirected from the liver to the small intestine. Since the gallbladder is no longer in use, bile is diluted. The initial consequence is a laxative effect that can produce diarrhea, but for most people, this will resolve on its own.

Nonsurgical therapies

If surgery is not an option, such as if the patient is very old, doctors can try a few additional methods to remove the gallstones.

Oral dissolving therapy combines the medicines ursodiol (Actigall) and chenodiol (Chenix) to break up gallstones. These drugs contain bile acids, which help to dissolve the stones. This procedure is ideal for breaking up cholesterol stones and can take months or years to work fully.

Another alternative is shock wave lithotripsy. A lithotripter is a machine that sends shock waves through a person's body. These shock waves can shatter gallstones into smaller pieces.

Percutaneous gallbladder drainage is performed by inserting a sterile needle into the gallbladder and aspirating (drawing out) bile. A tube is then placed to aid in further drainage. This operation isn't usually the first line of defense and is generally reserved for people who aren't candidates for other procedures.

Gallstone risk factors

Some gallstone risk factors are nutrition-related, whereas others are not as easily controlled. All uncontrollable risk factors are age, color, gender, and family history.

Risk factors in one's lifestyle

- Obesity diets are heavy in fat or cholesterol and lacking in fiber

- going through a quick weight loss

- having type 2 diabetes

- Factors of genetic risk

- being a woman of Native American or Mexican descent

- being 60+ years or more, having a family history of gallstones

- Medical danger signs

- surviving cirrhosis

- being pregnant and taking cholesterol-lowering drugs

- taking estrogen-containing medicines (like specific birth control)

While some medications may raise your risk of gallstones, don't stop taking them unless you've discussed them with your doctor and received their clearance.

Diagnosis

Your doctor will examine you physically, including assessing your eyes and skin for noticeable color changes. A yellowish tinge may indicate jaundice caused by excess bilirubin in your body.

Different tests that allow your doctor to look inside your body may be used during the checkup. Among these tests are:

Ultrasound. Your abdomen is imaged with an ultrasound. It is the preferred imaging approach for confirming gallstone disease. It may also reveal anomalies related to acute cholecystitis.

CT scan of the abdomen. This imaging examination photographs your liver and abdominal region.

Radionuclide scan of the gallbladder. This vital scan takes approximately one hour to complete. Radioactive material is injected into your veins by a professional. This chemical enters your bloodstream and travels to your liver and gallbladder. A scan may reveal indications of illness or bile duct blockage caused by stones.

Blood tests are performed. Your doctor might prescribe a blood test to check your bilirubin levels if they are concerned about you. Your liver's health and functionality can be determined by the tests as well.

CHAPTER 2 MODERATE DIET AND FOODS TO CONSUME

T try the following tips to assist improve your condition and lower your chance of gallstones:

- Consume fewer processed carbohydrates (such as cookies and white bread) and less sugar.

- Increase your diet of good fats, such as fish oil and olive oil, which may aid in the contraction and emptying of your gallbladder.

- Consume a limited amount of fiber daily (women need about 25 grams daily, and men need about 38 grams daily).

- Every day, engage in some form of physical activity.

- Maintain proper hydration.

- Lose weight gradually if you want to. Rapid weight loss may raise your chances of developing gallstones and other health issues.

Prevention

While there is no failsafe technique to prevent gallstones entirely, cholesterol does play a significant part in their production. You should reduce your intake of foods high in saturated fat. Among these meals are fatty meats such as sausage and bacon, cakes and cookies, lard and cream, and some cheeses.

Dietary Guidelines for a Healthy Gallbladder

Gallstones and cancer are two gallbladder disorders that can be avoided with dietary changes.

According to research, persons who eat a healthy diet have a lower chance of gallbladder disease.

Knowing which foods to eat and which to avoid can help the gallbladder stay healthy, especially for people who have gallstones or other gallbladder problems.

Although there is no recommended diet for a healthy gallbladder, following a few tips will help maintain the gallbladder healthy and operating correctly.

Foods to consume

The gallbladder diet seeks to alleviate the stress that diet can place on the gallbladder by simplifying digestion or supporting the gallbladder. A 2015 study looked at 114 ladies' food patterns and risk of gallstones.

The researchers defined two types of diets for this study:

Fresh fruits and green vegetables, fruit juice, low-fat dairy products, whole grains, nuts, spices, and legumes are all part of a healthy diet.

A diet high in processed meat, soft drinks, refined grains, red meat, high-fat products, high sugar, tea, fat, baked potato, snacks, egg, too much salt, pickled food, and sauerkraut is unhealthy.

People who ate a well-balanced diet were less likely to develop gallbladder disease.

Here are some specific foods to avoid to keep your gallbladder healthy.

Foods derived from plants

A nutritious diet will provide a wide range of nutrients. A diet rich in plant foods can supply the nutrients the body requires to stay healthy.

Vitamins, minerals, and antioxidants are abundant in plant-based meals. These may aid in the prevention of gallbladder disease.

Antioxidants are nutrients that aid in removing harmful chemicals known as free radicals from the body.

Lean protein

Protein is required for bodily tissue repair and growth. Red meat and dairy products are abundant in protein but also heavy in fat, which can stress the gallbladder.

Low-fat protein dishes are an excellent choice. They include:

- Poultry

- Fish

-

Low-fat items made from milk

- seeds and nuts

- soy and soy-related items

- legumes like beans and lentils

- Soy milk, for example, is a dairy substitute.

Added salt is commonly found in processed meats and dairy products. Fresh foods with no added sugar are a healthier option.

A 2016 study discovered a relationship between a high vegetable protein diet and a lower risk of gallbladder disease.

Fiber

Fiber, according to experts, promotes digestive health and may protect against gallbladder disease by increasing the passage of food through the stomach and decreasing the generation of secondary bile acids.

In 2014, researchers investigated how a high-fiber diet affects biliary sludge production during a quick weight-loss diet for obese patients. Biliary or gallbladder sludge is a material that increases the likelihood of gallbladder disease developing. It can accumulate in persons who fast or lose weight rapidly.

Those who ate a high-fiber diet developed less gallbladder sludge, lowering their risk of gallbladder disease. This shows that fiber may aid in preventing gallbladder disease in persons who need to reduce weight quickly and possibly permanently. Fruits, green vegetables, legumes, nuts, and seeds are all good sources of fiber:

- Complete grains

- Healthy fats

- Unsaturated fats, such as omega-3, may aid in gallbladder protection.

- Cold-water fish dry fruits, nuts, walnuts, and seeds such as flaxseeds.

People can also take different supplements, but they should consult a doctor first because some accessories are inappropriate for everyone.

Coffee

Coffee used in moderation may help safeguard gallbladder function. According to research, several compounds in coffee may have varied effects on gallbladder function, including balancing specific chemicals and boosting gallbladder and perhaps intestine activity.

Calcium

A sufficient calcium intake in the diet can benefit gallbladder health. Calcium can be found in dark, leafy greens like kale and broccoli. Dairy products, including yogurt, cheese, and milk dairy substitutes, added nutrients, such as almond or flax milk sardine and the juice of oranges. People who are predisposed to gallbladder disease should consume zero-fat dairy products.

Folate, magnesium, and vitamin C

Vitamin C, magnesium, and folate may all aid in the prevention of gallbladder disease:

- Citrus fruits and vegetables

-

kiwifruit

- broccoli

- strawberries

- tomatoes

Because vitamin C is a water-soluble vitamin, boiling in water may remove some of it from the meal. The most excellent sources are fresh, uncooked fruits and vegetables.

- Almonds and cashews contain magnesium.

- peanut butter and peanuts

- spinach beans, black beans, and edamame

- milk made from soy

- potato

- avocado

- rice

- yogurt

- banana

- Beef liver and spinach are high in folate.

- cereals enriched with black-eyed peas

- asparagus

Although supplements are available, obtaining nutrients from the diet is preferable. Before taking supplements, people should consult with their doctor.

Avoidance foods

Some foods may raise the risk of gallbladder problems like gallstones. Those who are concerned about the health of their gallbladder should avoid or limit the foods listed below.

Carbohydrate refinement

Carbohydrates are vital components in most people's diets, and unrefined carbohydrates, such as whole grains and oats, can give them.

Refined carbs, on the other hand, may raise the risk of gallbladder diseases. According to one study, eating 40 grams (g) or more of sugar per day quadrupled the incidence of gallstones with symptoms.

- Added sugars and sweeteners are carbs to limit or avoid.

- blanched flour

- different refined grains

- ready-made baked items, such as cookies and cakes

- chocolate and candy

Fats that are unhealthy

The gallbladder generates bile, which aids the body's digestion of lipids. A high-fat diet, particularly saturated and trans fats, may burden this mechanism more.

Researchers discovered that those who consume red, processed meats and eggs as part of an unhealthy diet are more likely to develop gallstones.

Unhealthy fats can be found in:

- red, fatty meats

-

  prepared meats

- other prepared foods

- dairy products with total fat

- foods that are fried

- numerous fast foods

- salad dressings and sauces already made

- baked goods and desserts already made

- chocolate and other sweets

- frozen yogurt

Following gallbladder removal

People who have had their gallbladders operated on can still process food, but for a few days or weeks after the procedure, they may need to make some adjustments to their diet. In the days immediately following an operation, a patient may be instructed by their attending physician to consume several smaller meals. Maintain a diet limited to low fat for a period of several weeks. It is in the patient's best interest to keep away from caffeine consumption if they are experiencing bloating, constipation, or any other digestive complaints.

Avoid foods that are spicy or fatty.

Avoid anything that aggravates your symptoms. Gradually increase the amount of organic fiber in your diet

Anyone who notices greasy or foamy stools should seek medical attention. A gallbladder cleanses, flushing or detox is a dietary trend that scientists have labeled "misleading."

According to proponents, it can reset the gallbladder, flush out gallstones, improve digestive health, and improve gallbladder function. For two weeks, consume a rigorous diet with apple juice, followed by Epsom salts and a blend of olive oil and citrus juice.

Experts warn that recommending this diet without sufficient evidence is risky. Many people claim to notice "stones" in their feces; however, the scientific examination has shown that they are clumps of oil and citrus juice. Anyone concerned about gallbladder disease should consult a physician.

CHAPTER 3 SIMPLE AND DELICIOUS NO-

GALLBLADDER RECIPES

Strawberry French Toast Casserole

Cooking Period: 50 minutes

Number of Portions: 8

Required Materials for Recipe:

- Eight pieces spelled flour bread, chopped
- 1 1/2 cups strawberries, chopped
- 2 and 1/4 cups almond milk
- 1-quarter cup almond butter
- One quarter tsp salt
- 1/3 cup agave syrup
- Two tablespoons of ground flax meal

Instructions for this recipe:

1. Put a casserole dish in your oven after you have reached the temperature of 350 degrees F. Meanwhile, you have already covered it with cooking spray and added some bread and some strawberries.

2. In a dish, combine milk, butter, sugar, and salt. 3. Pour over the bread and berry combination, then set aside for at least half an hour to settle.
3. Bake for 45-50 minutes. Allow to chill slightly, then serve.

Nutritional Analysis: 200 calories; 6 g fat; 30 g total carbs; 8 g protein

---

Quick Vegan Breakfast Burritos

Cooking Period: 30 minutes

Number of Portions: 2 burritos

Required Materials for Recipe:

- 1 and a half cups water
- 3-quarter cup quinoa, already cook
- 1-quarter cup cilantro, 1/2 onion,1 squash
- Two tablespoons of almond butter
- 1-quarter tsp of each pepper chili, cumin, and garlic powder, plus half Tsp salt
- One cup garbanzo bean
- 1/4 avocado
- Greens
- Two spelled flour tortillas
- 1/4 cup organic salsa

Instructions for this recipe:

1. Cut the onion into thick circles. Coat a saucepan with vegetable butter, then put shallots on one side of the pan and zucchini on the other. Season the meat, cover it, and cook it for five minutes on one side before turning it over and cooking it for another five minutes. Take it out and put it to the side.

2. Add the beans to a skillet and season them with garlic powder, cumin powder, and chile powder. Place the pan over medium heat. Once bubbles begin to appear, reduce heat.
3. In a dish, combine the avocado and the vegetables. The salad should be seasoned, then put aside. Add cilantro to grains and stir.
4. Add ingredients, guacamole, and salsa. Slice the sandwiches after they have been rolled up.

Nutritional Analysis: 285 calories; 17 g fat; 1 g total carbs; 30 g protein

---

Alkaline Omelet

Cooking Period: 5 minutes

Number of Portions: 1

Required Materials for Recipe:

- 1/4 cup garbanzo bean flour
- 1/3 cup water
- 1/4 tsp of each sweet basil, onion powder, sea salt, oregano, cayenne powder
- Same proportion of each vegetables (1/4 cup) Roma tomato, onion, sweet pepper, mushrooms
- Grapeseed Oil

Instructions for this recipe:

1. Combine the water and flour inside a dish, then add the ingredients and give it a good stir.
2. Pour some oil into the pan, warm it, and then cook for another 3–4 minutes after adding all of the vegetables.

3. Incorporate the flour combination and continue to cook (3–4 minutes).
4. Cook it for a few more minutes after you have flipped it. Enjoy!

Nutritional Analysis: 235 calories; 13 g fat; 10 g total carbs; 20 g protein

---

Banana-Ginger Pancakes

Cooking Period: 6 minutes

Number of Portions: 4

Required Materials for Recipe:

- One ¼ cups almond milk
- One ¼ cup spelled flour
- 1 ½ teaspoons ground ginger
- Two teaspoons of baking powder
- Two tablespoons of agave nectar
- One teaspoon of vanilla extract
- Two tablespoons of applesauce, unsweetened
- 1 cup mashed bananas
- ¼ teaspoon salt
- vegetable oil

Instructions for this recipe:

1. In an ample dish, combine the baking powder, flour, ground ginger, and salt.
2. In a different dish, put soy milk, agave nectar, vanilla extract, and applesauce.
3. Now incorporate bananas and unite both prepare.
4. Put a quarter cup of the mixture in the warm pan. When you see a few bubbles appearing on the surface of the

pancake, flip it. Cook for an additional two minutes after you have flipped the pancake. Pancakes should be cooked for two minutes per side.

5. Once done, serve.

Nutritional Analysis: 268 calories; 2.2 g fat; 57 g total carbs; 8.7 g protein

---

Overnight Coconut Quinoa

Cooking Period: 20 minutes

Number of Portions: 6

Required Materials for Recipe:

- ¼ cup chia seeds
- Half cup quinoa
- Just 1 cup unsweetened coconut milk
- Two teaspoons of vanilla extract
- ¼ teaspoon cinnamon
- ½ cup walnuts
- 1 ½ cups berries
- pinch of salt

Instructions for this recipe:

1. Mix the seeds of chia, coconut milk, quinoa, vanilla essence, cinnamon, and salt. Mix until well combined. Put in the refrigerator overnight after covering with plastic film.
2. Put it in a saucepan and leave cook for a total of a 12mins.
3. Decorate the top with hazelnuts and cherries.
4. Once done, serve..

Nutritional Analysis: 487 calories; 42 g fat; 25 g total carbs; 9 g protein

---

Blueberry Banana Pancakes with Chunky Apple Compote

Cooking Period: 10 minutes

Number of Portions: 4

Required Materials for Recipe:

- Three flax eggs, Six bananas
- Two teaspoons of baking powder
- 1 ½ cups rolled oats
- Two ¼ cups of blueberries
- ¼ teaspoon salt
- Five dates pitted
- Two apples
- One tablespoon of lemon juice
- ¼ teaspoon cinnamon powder

Instructions for this recipe:

1. Add
2. Fresh oats to your blender and then blend for 1 minute. Add flax eggs, bananas, baking powder, and salt to the blender. Pulse for 2 minutes.
3. Transfer it to a small glass bowl and add the blueberries. Let sit for 10 minutes.
4. Heat a saucepan and add a dollop of almond butter. Add a few spoons of the pancake mix and fry until golden at the bottom. Remove to a plate.
5. Core and chop apples. Add apples, dates, lemon juice, cinnamon powder, and a pinch of salt to a blender and two tablespoons of water. Blend well. Remove to a plate.
6. Serve pancakes with apple compote.

Nutritional Analysis: 490 calories; 13 g fat; 35 g total carbs; 22 g protein

---

Toast with Beans and Avocado

Cooking Period: 5 minutes

Number of Portions: 2

Required Materials for Recipe:

- 1 cup garbanzo beans
- Two spelled flour bread slices
- One avocado, sliced
- Salt, to taste
- white onion, sliced

Instructions for this recipe:

1. Toast the bread slices. Add avocado and beans on top.
2. Add onions and sprinkle salt over it.
3. Serve and enjoy!

Nutritional Analysis: 762 calories; 72 g fat; 13 g total carbs; 19 g protein

_____

Morning Muesli

Cooking Period: 35 minutes

Number of Portions: 11

Required Materials for Recipe:

- ½ cup amaranth oats
- 1 cup almond milk
- 1 tbsp almonds, sliced
- ½ cup apple, chopped
- Dash of cinnamon

Instructions for this recipe:

1. Mix all elements from the list except almonds and apples and refrigerate overnight.
2. Enjoy topped with almonds and apples!

Nutritional Analysis: 218 calories; 12 g fat; 25 g total carbs; 5 g protein

Warm and Nutty Cinnamon Quinoa

Cooking Period: 20 minutes

Number of Portions: 4

Required Materials for Recipe:

- One cup water, quinoa organic, almond or coconut milk (each)
- 2 cups blackberries
- 1/3 cup almonds, chopped and toasted
- 1/2 teaspoon cinnamon
- Four teaspoons of organic agave nectar

Instructions for this recipe:

1. After that, you have reached the high point of a boil, reduce the flame, cover using a lid and cook for fifteen minutes.
2. When it is ready and after adding the cinnamon and the strawberries, divide the mixture between the four dishes.
3. After adding the almonds, drizzle each dish with one spoonful of agave nectar. Serve, and have fun!

Nutritional Analysis: 298 calories; 19 g fat; 16 g total carbs; 17 g protein

---

Quinoa Breakfast Patties

Cooking Period: 25 minutes

Number of Portions: 8

Required Materials for Recipe:

- 2 mugs vegetable broth
- Just 1 cup quinoa, already cooked
- Two flax eggs
- Two teaspoons parsley
- Two tablespoons Coconut Oil

- Salt - pepper

Instructions for this recipe:

1. Give the quinoa a thorough washing, and then add it to a skillet along with the vegetable stock. When it reaches a boil, reduce the flame and allow it simmers for 15 minutes.

2. Incorporate the quinoa, flax eggs, parsley, and two tablespoons of oil, salt, and pepper by thoroughly combining all of the ingredients.
3. Coat the bottom of the skillet with a touch of coco oil. After forming the mixture into spheres, position them on the pan and use the back of your hand to press them down. Cook for 3 minutes per side.
4. Sprinkle some parsley on top, and then serve. Enjoy!

Nutritional Analysis: 225 calories; 6 g fat; 52 g total carbs; 9 g protein

_____

Squash Breakfast Bowl

Cooking Period: 1 hour 25 minutes

Number of Portions: 2

Required Materials for Recipe:

- 16 oz. squash
- Two tablespoons of almond butter
- Two tablespoons almonds, chopped
- Cinnamon, to taste

Instructions for this recipe:

1. Warm your oven (400° F). Mash squash using a fork and wrap in foil. Bake for 15 minutes. Let cool, peel, and chop.
2. Mash the squash in a bowl, and add cinnamon. Add to a bowl and top with nuts. Add almond butter. Serve and enjoy!

Nutritional Analysis: 445 calories; 35 g fat; 19 g total carbs; 14 g protein

Parsley Kale and Berry Smoothie

Cooking Period: 5 minutes

Number of Portions: 1

Required Materials for Recipe:

- One banana, cut into pieces
- 1/2 cup flat-leaf parsley (leaves & stems), packed
- One teaspoon of ground flaxseed
- Four kale leaves, center ribs removed
- 1 cup water

- 1 cup organic berries, frozen

Instructions for this recipe:

1. Add all the specific ingredients for the smoothie to a blender and puree until you add more water if too thick.
2. Pour into chilled glasses and serve immediately. Enjoy!

Nutritional Analysis: 214 calories; 2.4 g fat; 49 g total carbs; 4 g protein

---

Quinoa Bowl with Avocado

Cooking Period: 15 minutes

Number of Portions: 4

Required Materials for Recipe:

- One tablespoon of olive oil
- One teaspoon turmeric
- Four servings of quinoa, cooked
- One avocado
- Two tablespoons of almond butter
- salt and pepper, to taste

Instructions for this recipe:

1. Cook quinoa according to package directions. Add butter and divide among four bowls.
2. Add 1/4 avocado and 1/4 tomato to each bowl. Season and serve.

Nutritional Analysis: 311 calories; 16 g fat; 42 g total carbs; 13 g protein

---

Green Apple Smoothie

Cooking Period: 5 minutes

Number of Portions: 1

Required Materials for Recipe:

- 4 Medrol dates
- One green apple
- 3 cups spinach
- ½ cup water
- One teaspoon of lemon juice
- Eight ice cubes

Instructions for this recipe:

1. Core the apple and slice it into chunks. Remove pits from dates.
2. Insert all of the listed ingredients in a blender and process until smooth.
3. Enjoy!

Nutritional Analysis: 210 calories; 3 g fat; 7 g total carbs; 3 g protein

---

Creamed Turnips and Greens

Cooking Period: 20 minutes

Number of Portions: 6

Required Materials for Recipe:

- One lb. turnips
- Four cups turnip greens, chopped
- Two tablespoons of extra-virgin olive oil
- ½ cup water
- Two tablespoons of spelled Flour
- 1 and a half cups almond milk
- Half tsp nutmeg and a pinch white pepper
- Salt, to taste

Instructions for this recipe:

1. Warm the oil in a saucepan. Turnips, water, and salt should be added before the pot is covered and brought to a simmer.
2. After you have added the vegetables, you should continue to cook (about 15 mins). If the leaves start to adhere together, add a little bit more water.
3. After adding the flour, raise the temperature and continue cooking for another thirty seconds. Milk, cinnamon, white pepper, and additional salt should be added to the dish. Cook for three to four minutes while swirling the pan frequently. Serve with the juice of one lemon on top (if you prefer).

Nutritional Analysis: 243 calories; 17 g fat; 5 g total carbs; 17 g protein

---

Breakfast Hash

Cooking Period: 1 hour

Number of Portions: 6

Required Materials for Recipe:

- Three squash diced
- One teaspoon of dried thyme
- 1 quarter cup olive oil
- One onion, diced
- Salt - pepper

Instructions for this recipe:

1. Combine squash, oil, spices and mix well. Bake at 450 F (fifteen minutes). Stir every 5 minutes.
2. In an oiled skillet, cook onion (8 minutes). Season to taste.
3. Add squash to the onion mixture and mix well to combine. Cook for 1-2 minutes.
4. Serve and enjoy.

Nutritional Analysis: 202 calories; 13 g fat; 12 g total carbs; 10 g protein

Kale, Tahini, and Bell Pepper Wraps

Cooking Period: 10 minutes

Number of Portions: 2

Required Materials for Recipe:

- Two spelled flour tortillas
- Half cup tahini
- One sweet pepper, sliced
- Just 1 cup kale

Instructions for this recipe:

1. Spread tahini on top of each tortilla.
2. Top with the remaining ingredients and roll into burritos. Secure with toothpicks and serve.

Nutritional Analysis: 209 calories; 11 g fat; 15 g total carbs; 18 g protein

Breakfast Kamut

Cooking Period: 5 minutes

Number of Portions: 2

Required Materials for Recipe:

- 1 cup (7 oz) Kamut berries, milled
- 3 3/4 cups almond milk
- 1 half teaspoon salt
- One tablespoon almond butter
- Four tablespoons of agave syrup

Instructions for this recipe:

1. Combine Kamut, almond milk, and salt, and mix to incorporate. Warm and reach a high point a boil, then reduce the flame and keep on for about 10 minutes.
2. When ready, mix well in the butter and agave nectar and serve.

Nutritional Analysis: 194 calories; 11 g fat; 10 g total carbs; 14 g protein

---

Creamy Vanilla Matcha Amaranth

Cooking Period: 20 minutes

Number of Portions: 2

Required Materials for Recipe:

- 1 ½ cup water
- ½ cup amaranth
- ¼ cup almond milk

- ½ teaspoon vanilla extract
- One teaspoon of matcha powder
- One tablespoon of agave syrup
- One tablespoon of hemp seeds
- pinch of salt

Instructions for this recipe:

1. Bring a boiling the water.
2. Incorporate amaranth and salt, and let cooking just 15 minutes.
3. Eliminate the pan from the flame and pour in the almond milk, the matcha powder, the vanilla essence, and the agave nectar. Combine everything very thoroughly.
4. Should put half of the mixture in each of the two dishes, apply on each hemp seed, and serve.

Nutritional Analysis: 240 calories; 11 g fat; 31 g total carbs; 5 g protein

_____

Blackberry Breakfast Bars

Cooking Period: 20 minutes

Number of Portions: 8

Required Materials for Recipe:

- Four baby bananas
- 2 cups quinoa
- 1 cup spelled flour
- ½ cup grapeseed oil
- ¼ cup agave nectar
- ¼ teaspoon sea salt
- Organic blackberry jam

Instructions for this recipe:

1. Preheat your oven to 350°F. Meanwhile mash baby bananas in a plate.
2. Add grapeseed oil plus agave nectar to bananas and mix well.
3. Add quinoa, sea salt, and spelled flour. Mix well until dough is formed. Press it into a baking pan.
4. Add jam on top and crumble the remaining dough on top.
5. Bake for 20 minutes and serve!

Nutritional Analysis: 471 calories; 16 g fat; 76 g total carbs; 6 g protein

---

Cardamom and Apple Quinoa Porridge

Cooking Period: 20 minutes

Number of Portions: 2

Required Materials for Recipe:

- 1 cup quinoa
- Four cardamom pods
- Two apples, cut into slices
- One teaspoon of agave syrup
- 8 1/2 oz. almond milk

Instructions for this recipe:

1. Add cardamom and quinoa to a pan with 9 oz. Water and 3 1/2 oz. Milk.

1. Incorporate the remaining milk and cook for just 5 minutes. Remove the cardamom pods, divide the mixture among bowls and add peaches and agave syrup. Serve and enjoy.

Nutritional Analysis: 501 calories; 10 g fat; 23 g total carbs; 17 g protein

---

Arugula and Avocado Breakfast Sandwich

Cooking Period: 20 minutes

Number of Portions: 2

Required Materials for Recipe:

- ¼ cup almond yogurt
- Four slices spelled flour bread, toasted
- 1 cup arugula
- One avocado, peeled, pitted, and sliced
- One tablespoon pepitas
- salt and pepper

Instructions for this recipe:

1. Season yogurt with salt and pepper.
2. Place two bread slices on two plates. Add an even layer of yogurt sauce to the toast.
3. Add a portion of arugula and avocado on top, along with pepitas. Top with another bread slice. Slice sandwich.
4. Once done, serve.

Nutritional Analysis: 131 calories; 5 g fat; 14 g total carbs; 8 g protein

---

Cinnamon and Almond Porridge

Cooking Period: 10 minutes

Number of Portions: 4

Required Materials for Recipe:

- Two cups of each amaranth, almond milk, water
- Two Tsp of agave syrup
- ¼ teaspoon vanilla extract
- ½ cup almonds

- ½ teaspoon ground cinnamon
- ¼ teaspoon salt

Instructions for this recipe:

1. Combine all ingredients (except almonds and cinnamon) to a pan and stir well. Cook for just 5 minutes, stirring often.
2. Add almonds and cinnamon on top.
3. Once done, serve.

Nutritional Analysis: 239 calories; 11 g fat; 44 g total carbs; 10 g protein

---

Green Almond Smoothie

Preparation time: 5 minutes

Number of Portions: 1

Required Materials for Recipe:

- One banana, One mug coconut milk
- ¼ cup protein in powder
- Two tablespoons almond (butter)
- 2 mugs kale, One mug ice

Instructions for this recipe:

1. Add all the specific ingredients for the smoothie to a blender and create a smooth compost.
2. When ready, you can serve. Enjoy!

Nutritional Analysis: 238 calories; 15.8 g fat; 8 g total carbs; 14 g protein

---

Almond Flour Muffins

Cooking Period: 30 minutes

Number of Portions: 12

Required Materials for Recipe:

- 1 cup blanched almond flour
- Two flax eggs
- One tablespoon of agave nectar
- ¼ tsp baking soda, Half tsp apple cider vinegar

Instructions for this recipe:

1. Mix soda and flour. The flax eggs, nectar, and vinegar should be mixed in a distinct bowl.
2. Combine both mixtures and turned well.
3. When you have reached the temperature of 350 F in your oven, you can pour the mixture into muffin tins and bake for 15 minutes. Enjoy!

Nutritional Analysis: 555 calories; 2 g fat; 115 g total carbs; 16 g protein

---

Roasted Red Rose Potatoes and Kale Breakfast Hash

Cooking Period: 45 minutes

Number of Portions: 2

Required Materials for Recipe:

- Two tablespoons of coconut oil
- Two red rose potatoes
- One teaspoon of coconut sugar
- Same quantity for each 1 onion, bundle of kale
- 1/8 tsp turmeric
- ½ teaspoon each salt and pepper
- Two tablespoons of fresh parsley

Instructions for this recipe:

1. Coat potatoes and onion in a mixture of a half tablespoon of oil, coconut sugar, a sprinkle each of salt and pepper, and stir to combine.
2. Cook the onion and potatoes in the oven for thirty-five minutes, turning them over halfway through. Remove from oven and put aside.
3. Put the pressed tofu in a dish and break it up into smaller chunks with your hands. To season, add a teaspoon each of salt and pepper, along with turmeric and chopped parsley. Set aside at this moment.
4. Warm a pan. Include the tofu with a half teaspoonful of oil and one teaspoon of tandoori masala seasoning. Continue to turn occasionally while cooking for another 5 minutes. Remove from saucepan and put aside.
5. Place the kale in a little casserole with the olive oil that you just added. Add one spoonful of tandoori masala seasoning, along with some salt and pepper, before serving.
6. Now you are ready to serve: put an equal amount of kale on each of the two dishes, then cover with potatoes and onion. Sprinkle the remaining chopped parsley on top. Serve.

Nutritional Analysis: 355 calories; 15.7 g fat; 37.3 g total carbs; 15.7 g protein

---

Date and Almond Porridge

Cooking Period: 10 minutes

Number of Portions: 1

Required Materials for Recipe:

- 1 Medjool date, chopped
- Six ¾ oz. almond milk
- One teaspoon of almond butter
- ½ cup buckwheat flakes
- ¼ cup strawberries, hulled

Instructions for this recipe:

1. Add the date and milk to a pan. Heat gently and add the buckwheat flakes and cook for a few minutes.
2. Add in butter and top with strawberries. Serve.

Nutritional Analysis: 306 calories; 10.7 g fat; 47 g total carbs; 10 g protein

---

Almond Biscuits

Cooking Period: 25 minutes

Number of Portions: 8

Required Materials for Recipe:

- 1 cup almond milk
- Two cups almond flour
- 1 tbsp baking powder, lemon juice (each)
- Half teaspoon baking soda

- A pinch of salt
- Four tablespoons of almond butter

Instructions for this recipe:

1. Put a tin in the oven already preheat (to 455 degrees F.) while also greasing it with oil.
2. In a dish, combine all of the dry ingredients. After adding butter, thoroughly combine the ingredients to form granules.
3. Add all of the ingredients that contain liquid and mix them together thoroughly. Knead the dough for seven to ten minutes.
4. Form into biscuits and roast for 10 to 15 minutes on a cookie sheet.

Nutritional Analysis: 360 calories; 27.3 g fat; 10 g total carbs; 19 g protein

---

Red rose potato Toasts

Cooking Period: 15 minutes

Number of Portions: 8-10

Required Materials for Recipe:

- One tablespoon of avocado oil
- Two red rose potatoes, sliced
- One teaspoon salt

Instructions for this recipe:

1. Get a baking sheet ready and turn the oven on to 425 degrees Fahrenheit.
2. Spread the potato slices on the parchment paper, leaving some room between them, and grease both sides with the avocado oil.

3. Season with salt. Put it in the oven for 5 to 6 minutes, flip it over, and bake for another 5 minutes. Enjoy!

Nutritional Analysis: 215 calories;6 g fat; 10 g total carbs; 9 g protein

Vegetable Rose Potato

Cooking Period: 20 minutes

Number of Portions: 4

Required Materials for Recipe:

- Four red rose potatoes
- Six leaves of Lacinato kale, stemmed, chopped
- Two tablespoons oil
- One of each onion, sweet pepper
- One tsp of smoked paprika
- One teaspoon of seasoning, salt-free
- Ground pepper, and salt, to taste

Instructions for this recipe:

1. Microwave the fresh potatoes until done but still firm. Finely chop them when cool.

2. In an oiled skillet, sauté onion for just 2 mins, then incorporate potatoes and sweet pepper, mix, and cook until their color is golden brown.
3. Add in the kale and seasoning, then cook, constantly stirring, until the mixture is a bit browned. Occasionally add water to prevent sticking if necessary.
4. Sprinkle with pepper and salt to taste. Serve hot.

Nutritional Analysis: 337 calories; 7.4 g fat; 63 g total carbs; 8 g protein

---

Kale Brussels Sprouts Salad

Cooking Period: 20 minutes

Number of Portions: 2

Required Materials for Recipe:

- One bunch of curly green kale stems removed, chopped
- ¼ cup almonds, sliced
- ½ lb. Brussels sprouts, shredded
- Two teaspoons of white miso
- ¼ cup tahini
- Two tablespoons of white wine vinegar
- Two teaspoons of agave syrup
- ¼ cup water
- A pinch of red pepper, salt

Instructions for this recipe:

1. Season kale with salt and drizzle with salt. Massage until kale becomes darker in color. Transfer kale to a bowl.
2. Whisk vinegar, tahini, agave syrup, miso, and pepper in a bowl.
3. Whisk in the water until creamy, then add this dressing over sprouts and kale.
4. Toast almonds in a pan until fragrant.
5. Add toasted almonds to the salad and toss. Once done, serve and enjoy.

Nutritional Analysis: 411 calories; 26.5 g fat; 33 g total carbs; 18 g protein

---

Rice Arugula Salad

Cooking Period: 7 minutes

Number of Portions: 2

Required Materials for Recipe:

- 1 cup wild rice, cooked
- One handful of arugula washed
- ¾ cup almonds
- Six sun-dried tomatoes in oil, chopped
- Three tablespoons of olive oil
- One onion
- Pepper and salt, to taste

Instructions for this recipe:

1. Roast almonds for 3 minutes in a skillet. Place in salad dish.
2. Sauté onions in 1/3 olive oil for 3 minutes. Cook dried tomatoes for 2 minutes. Put in a dish.
3. Fry the bread in the leftover olive oil until crispy. Sprinkle salt and pepper. Put away.
4. Mix aragula into sautéed tomato mélange. Mix in wild rice. Salt and pepper and serve.

Nutritional Analysis: 688 calories; 37.7 g fat; 56 g total carbs; 19 g protein

———————————

Tomato Salad

Cooking Period: 15 minutes

Number of Portions: 4

Required Materials for Recipe:

- One head of romaine lettuce, washed, chopped
- One avocado, sliced
- 24 cherry tomatoes
- ½ cup cilantro, chopped
- Fresh lime juice for dressing

Instructions for this recipe:

1. Combine all the ingredients in an ample bowl. Garnish with lime juice dressing.
2. Toss well to combine, then divide in a 4 plates. Enjoy immediately.

Nutritional Analysis: 203 calories; 16.2 g fat; 12 g total carbs; 6 g protein

---

Kale Apple Roasted Root Vegetable Salad

Cooking Period: 30 minutes

Number of Portions: 6

Required Materials for Recipe:

- 1 ½ cups parsnips, turnips, and red rose potatoes, diced
- 8 cups kale, chopped
- ½ cup apple chunks
- Two tablespoons of apple cider vinegar
- ½ teaspoon cinnamon
- ½ teaspoon turmeric
- Four tablespoons of olive oil
- Salt and pepper

Instructions for this recipe:

1. Warm a pan. Vinegar, apple, cinnamon, curcumin, and salt should be boiled. Set away the boiling liquid.
2. Preheat your oven to 350 F.
3. Carrots, turnips, and red rose potatoes in an oiled pan go roast for 10 minutes in the oven, already warm.
4. In an extra pan with olive oil, cook kale and pears for just 4 minutes
5. Unite both mixtures and cook for another five mins.
6. Salted, peppered, and enjoy hot!

Nutritional Analysis: 128 calories; 16 g fat; 32 g total carbs; 3 g protein

---

Rice Arugula Salad with Sesame Garlic Dressing

Cooking Period: 1 hour

Number of Portions: 4

Required Materials for Recipe:

- 1 cup wild rice, cooked
- 1/8 teaspoon cumin
- ½ bunch of arugula, chopped
- Two tablespoons parsley, chopped
- Two tablespoons basil, chopped
- Salt and black pepper to taste

For the dressing:

- One head of garlic, roasted and peeled
- ½ cup apple juice
- ¼ cup lemon juice
- ¼ cup tahini
- ¼ cup virgin olive oil

- Salt, to taste

Instructions for this recipe:

1. Blend all sauce ingredients until smooth and creamy. Set away.
2. Heat a stockpot. Cumin and salt rice. Rest for 10 minutes.
3. Add greens, parsley, basil, olives, salt, and pepper to the dish. Have fun!

Nutritional Analysis: 447 calories; 44.4 g fat; 43 g total carbs; 19 g protein

---

Roasted Lemon Asparagus Watercress Salad

Cooking Period: 10 minutes

Number of Portions: 4

Required Materials for Recipe:

- 2 cups asparagus, ends trimmed
- 2 cups watercress
- 2 cups baby spinach

- One lemon, sliced, seeded
- One onion, sliced
- 1/8 teaspoon cayenne
- Two tablespoons of olive oil, Salt, pepper

Instructions for this recipe:

1. Olive oil should be heated. Cook for approximately five minutes after adding the cleaned asparagus. Set aside.
2. Place the saucepan back over on a heat setting of medium-low. Include the remaining olive oil in the recipe.
3. Cook for approximately 5 minutes after adding the onion and lemon segments. Remove the dish from the heat and season it with salt, pepper, and cayenne pepper.
4. Include the broccoli in the contents of a large dish. The onion that has been prepared and the lemon segments should be added on top. After everything else, add the asparagus.
5. Serve, and have fun!!

Nutritional Analysis: 129 calories; 7 g fat; 11 g total carbs; 5 g protein

Pumpkin and Brussels Sprouts Mix

Cooking Period: 35 minutes

Number of Portions: 8

Required Materials for Recipe:

- 1 lb. Brussels sprouts halved
- One pumpkin, peeled, cubed
- Four garlic cloves, sliced
- Two tablespoons of fresh parsley, chopped
- Liquid: Two tbsp balsamic vinegar, 1/3 cup olive oil
- Salt - pepper

Instructions for this recipe:

1. Preheat your oven. Be sure to spray your baking dish entirely with cooking spray before beginning.
2. Combine pumpkin seeds, garlic, and sprouts I. Pour oil over the vegetables and toss to coat.
3. Transfer to the baking dish and cook for 35-40 minutes. Stir once halfway.
4. Serve topped with parsley.

Nutritional Analysis: 152 calories; 9 g fat; 17 g carbohydrate; 4 g protein

---

Almond and Tomato Salad

Cooking Period: 12 minutes

Number of Portions: 4

Required Materials for Recipe:

- 1 cup arugula/ rocket
- 7 oz fresh tomatoes, sliced or chopped
- Two teaspoons of olive oil
- 2 cups kale
- 1/2 cup almonds

Instructions for this recipe:

1. Add and heat olive oil.
2. Add tomatoes and fry for about Ten Minutes. Once cooked, allow it to cool.
3. Incorporate all fresh ingredients and serve.

Nutritional Analysis: 355 calories; 19.1 g fat; 8.3 g carbohydrate; 33 g protein; 135 mg sodium; 2 g fiber

---

Strawberry Spinach Salad

Cooking Period: 10 minutes

Number of Portions: 4

Required Materials for Recipe:

- 5 cups of baby spinach
- 2 cups strawberries, sliced
- Two tablespoons lemon, only juice
- Half tsp Dijon mustard, 1/4 cup olive oil
- 3/4 cup toasted almonds
- 1-quarter onion
- Salt - pepper

Instructions for this recipe:

1. Take a large bowl, mix Dijon mustard, juice of 2 lemon, oil and combine. Now season the mixture using pepper and salt.
2. Mix strawberries, half a cup of almonds, and sliced onion in a bowl.
3. Pour dressing on top and toss to combine. Serve the salad topped with almonds and vegan cheese.

Nutritional Analysis: 116 calories; 3 g fat; 13 g total carbs; 6 g protein

---

Apple Spinach Salad

Cooking Period: 10 minutes

Number of Portions: 4

Required Materials for Recipe:

- 5 ounces of fresh spinach
- 1/4 red onion, sliced
- One apple, sliced
- 1/4 cup sliced toasted almonds

For the Dressing:

- Three tablespoons of red wine vinegar
- 1/3 cup olive oil
- One minced garlic clove
- Two teaspoons of Dijon mustard
- Salt, and pepper, to taste

Instructions for this recipe:

1. Combine wine vinegar, olive oil, garlic, and Dijon mustard in a bowl. Season with black pepper and salt.
2. Mix fresh spinach, apple, onion, and toasted almonds in a separate bowl. Pour the new dressing on top and toss to combine. Serve

Nutritional Analysis: 232 calories; 20.8 g fat; 10 g total carbs; 3 g protein

———————————————

Kale Power Salad

Cooking Period: 40 minutes

Number of Portions: 2

Required Materials for Recipe:

- One bunch of kale, ribs removed and chopped
- 1/2 cup quinoa
- One tablespoon of olive oil
- 1/2 lime, juiced
- ½ teaspoon salt
- One tablespoon of olive oil
- One red rose potato, cut into small cubes
- One teaspoon cumin
- 3-quarter teaspoons salt, Half teaspoon paprika
- One lime, juiced
- One avocado, sliced into long strips
- One tablespoon of olive oil
- One tablespoon of cilantro leaves
- One jalapeno, deseeded, membranes removed and chopped
- salt
- ¼ cup pepitas

Instructions for this recipe:

1. Quinoa needs to be rinsed for two minutes in a strainer placed over a sink filled with flowing water.
2. Add quinoa that has been rinsed to a saucepan that has been filled with two cups of water. Cook the mixture at a medium simmer for fifteen minutes. Remove the quinoa from the heat and place a cover on it, allowing it to sit for five minutes. Take off the cover, then use a spatula to fluff the quinoa while you wait for the surplus water to evaporate. Put away to settle down.
3. In a saucepan set over a heat setting medium, prepare the olive oil. At this stage, the crimson rose potatoes need to be added and mixed in with everything else.
4. Add smoked paprika, cumin, and salt. Combine in order to incorporate.

5. Once the skillet is hot and bubbling, pour in a quarter cup of water. Cover it and bring the heat down. Continue cooking for another 10 minutes while swirling the pan periodically. Remove the cover from the skillet, adjust the heat so that it is medium, and continue cooking for another 7 minutes. Put to the side to settle down.
6. Place the kale in a dish, sprinkle it with salt, and massage it thoroughly with your palms. Repeat the process of crushing large handfuls of kale in your palms until the kale becomes a deeper color.
7. In a dish, combine one lime juice, one-half teaspoon of salt, and two tablespoons of olive oil. After adding, stir the greens to evenly distribute the dressing.
8. Place two avocados, two lime liquids, and two tablespoons of olive oil, jalapeño, cilantro leaves, and salt in a blender. Blend until smooth. Serve immediately. Mix the avocado puree well, then add the seasoning.
9. Place pepitas in a saucepan and toast them for five minutes over medium-low heat, flipping them frequently.
    10. 10.
    Put the quinoa in the dish with the spinach, and mix everything together thoroughly. The kale and quinoa combination should be distributed evenly among the four containers.
    11.11.
    Garnish with pepitas, avocado salsa, and red rose potatoes. Enjoy!

Nutritional Analysis: 250 calories; 11 g fat; 25 g total carbs; 9 g protein

---

Falafel Kale Salad with Tahini Dressing

Cooking Period: 5 minutes
Number of Portions: 4
Required Materials for Recipe:

- 12 balls Vegan Falafels
- 6 cups kale, chopped
- 1/2 red onion, thinly sliced
- Two slices of pita bread, cut into squares
- One jalapeño, chopped
- Tahini Dressing
- 1-2 lemons, juiced

Instructions for this recipe:

1. In a mixing bowl, combine kale and lemon juice and toss well to mix. Place into the refrigerator.
2. Divide kale among four bowls. Top with three Falafel balls, red onion, jalapeño, and pita slices.
3. Top with tahini dressing and serve.

Nutritional Analysis: 178 calories; 2.8 g fat; 16 g total carbs; 4 g protein

----

Fig and Kale Salad

Cooking Period: 15 minutes

Number of Portions: 2

Required Materials for Recipe:

- One ripe avocado
- Two tablespoons of lemon juice
- 3 ½ oz kale, packed, stems removed, and cut into large-sized bits
- One carrot, shredded

- One yellow zucchini, diced
- Four fresh figs
- ¼ cup ground flaxseed
- 1 cup mixed green leaves
- One teaspoon of sea salt

Instructions for this recipe:

1. Combine kale, avocado, lemon juice, and sea salt. Massage together until kale wilts.
2. Add in zucchini, carrot, and 2 cups of mixed green leaves.
3. Fold in figs and remaining ingredients. Toss and serve.

Nutritional Analysis: 255 calories; 12.5 g fat; 35 g total carbs; 6 g protein

---

Cucumber Avocado Toast

Cooking Period: 5 minutes

Number of Portions: 2

Required Materials for Recipe:

- One cucumber, sliced
- Two sprouted (Essene) bread slices, toasted
- ¼ handful of basil leaves, chopped
- Four tablespoons avocado, mashed
- Salt - pepper
- One teaspoon of lemon, but only juice

Instructions for this recipe:

1. Combine lemon juice with the mashed avocado, then spread the mixture on two bread slices.
2. Top with cucumber slices along with the finely chopped basil leaves. Generously sprinkle with salt and pepper, and enjoy!

Nutritional Analysis: 232 calories; 14 g fat; 24 g total carbs; 5 g protein

_____

Kale and Cucumber Salad

Cooking Period: 60 minutes

Number of Portions: 2

Required Materials for Recipe:

- One garlic clove
- 3 ½ oz fresh ginger
- 1/2 green Thai chili
- In the same measurement use 1 and a half tbsp sugar, fish sauce, vegetable oil
- 1 English cucumber, thinly sliced
- One bunch of Red Russian kale, 1 Persian cucumber
- Two tablespoons of fresh lime juice
- One small red onion, sliced
- One teaspoon sugar
- Two tablespoons of cilantro, chopped
- Salt, to taste

Instructions for this recipe:

1. Preheat the broiler and broil the ginger with the peel on for fifty minutes, rotating it once during that time. After it has cooled, divide it.
2. In a processor, combine the pepper, ginger, garlic, sugar, fish sauce, oil, and two tablespoons of water until a paste is formed.
3. Place a quarter cup of the vinaigrette and the kale in a dish, and toss to coat. Kale can be made more tender by massaging it with your palms.

4. In a dish, combine Persian and English cucumbers, lime juice, onion, and sugar. Season with salt. Let it rest for 10 minutes.
5. Place the cucumber combination in a separate dish and add it to the bowl containing the kale. Toss to incorporate.
6. Sprinkle some cilantro on top, and serve.

Nutritional Analysis: 160 calories; 8 g fat; 22 g total carbs; 3 g protein

---

Mexican Quinoa

Cooking Period: 25 minutes

Number of Portions: 4

Required Materials for Recipe:

- 1 cup quinoa, uncooked and rinsed
- 1 ½ cup vegetable broth
- 3 cups diced tomatoes
- 2 cups frozen corn
- 1 cup fresh parsley, chopped
- One onion, chopped
- Three cloves of garlic, minced
- Two bell peppers, chopped
- One tablespoon of paprika powder

- ½ tablespoon cumin
- Two tbsp of each oil olive, lime juice
- Two green onions, chopped
- salt and pepper

Instructions for this recipe:

1. Put a large saucepan on the stove and turn the heat to medium. Add olive oil. Keep the shallots cooking for three minutes.
2. After adding the garlic and chilies, continue to simmer for another 5 minutes.
3. Include the remaining ingredients, including lime juice, green scallions, and cilantro, in the dish. Cook for approximately twenty minutes with the lid on. Maintain constant vigilance to prevent the quinoa from becoming stuck or charred.
4. Mix in some lime juice, sliced green scallions, and chopped cilantro.

Nutritional Analysis: 231 calories; 17.8 g fat; 19 g total carbs; 2 g protein

Mediterranean Parsley Salad

Cooking Period: 15 minutes

Number of Portions: 2

Required Materials for Recipe:

- ½ red onion, thinly sliced
- 1 cups parsley, chopped
- 1 Roma tomato, seeded and diced
- Six mints, chopped
- Three tablespoons of currants died
- One green chili, minced
- One tablespoon lemon
- Two tablespoons of olive oil
- 1/8 teaspoon sumac

- 1 quarter tsp pepper and salt

Instructions for this recipe:

1. Mix lemon juice, olive oil, sumac, salt, and pepper and whisk to combine well.
2. Toss parsley with the remaining ingredients in a separate bowl.
3. Add oil mixture to it and toss well and serve.

Nutritional Analysis: 110 calories; 8 g fat; 7 g total carbs; 1 g protein

---

Tomatoes Parsley Salad

Cooking Period: 10 minutes

Number of Portions: 2

Required Materials for Recipe:

- 2 cups curly parsley leaves, packed
- One teaspoon of garlic, minced
- 3-quarter cup sundried tomatoes
- Two tbsp of olive oil
- ½ cup basil leaves
- Two tablespoons of rice vinegar
- One shallot, one garlic, salt, pepper

Instructions for this recipe:

1. Clean the parsley, pat it dry, and place it in a dish. Garlic and tomatoes should be added. Toss thoroughly.
2. After washing the cilantro, allow it to air. Add it to a processor and add vinegar, oil, salt, and pepper. Combine until there are no lumps.
3. The vinaigrette should be seasoned with garlic and scallions.

4. Pour the vinaigrette over the lettuce, then give it a good toss. Place equal portions on each of the six lettuce dishes, and serve.

Nutritional Analysis: 245 calories; 19.8 g fat; 12 g total carbs; 7 g protein

---

Lemon Parsley Quinoa Salad

Cooking Period: 30 minutes

Number of Portions: 2

Required Materials for Recipe:

- One tablespoon of lemon juice
- 3 cups quinoa, cooked
- 1-quarter cup olive oil, 1 and half teaspoon lemon zest, one cup Italian flat-leaf parsley
- ½ bell pepper, diced
- Salt - black pepper

Instructions for this recipe:

1. Cook quinoa according to package instructions. Add some water and heat in a microwave.
2. Mix lemon juice and zest in a little bowl and whisk in olive oil, salt, and pepper.
3. Add parsley, rice, and diced pepper. Mix well and Enjoy!

Nutritional Analysis: 207 calories; 9 g fat; 28 g total carbs; 2.6 g protein

---

Quinoa and Parsley Salad

Cooking Period: 25 minutes

Number of Portions: 2

Required Materials for Recipe:

- ½ cup quinoa, uncooked
- 1 cup water
- ¾ cup parsley leaves
- ½ cup celery, sliced
- ½ cup green onions, sliced
- Three tablespoons of fresh lemon juice
- ½ cup dried apricots, chopped
- One tablespoon of agave syrup
- One tablespoon of olive oil
- ¼ cup unsalted pumpkinseed kernels, toasted
- Half tsp salt, pepper (half of each)

Instructions for this recipe:

1. In a pot, combine uncooked quinoa with water, and then bring to a simmer. Cover the pot, bring the heat down, and let it simmer for twenty minutes. Place in a dish and use a spatula to give it a fluffy texture.
2. Put in the chopped apricots, celery, parsley, and scallions.
3. Whisk olive oil, lemon juice, sugar, salt, and black pepper. Mix thoroughly after adding to the quinoa concoction.
4. Sprinkle some seeds on top, and serve.

Nutritional Analysis: 238 calories; 8.6 g fat; 35 g total carbs; 6 g protein

---

Summer Parsley Salad

Cooking Period: 5 minutes

Number of Portions: 2

Required Materials for Recipe:

- One bunch of parsley, One tomato, One sweet pepper
- Four baby cucumbers
- Two tbsp of olive oil
- Just 1 tablespoon of each lemon juice, white vinegar, agave syrup
- One teaspoon salt

Instructions for this recipe:

1. Add peppers, cucumbers, tomato, olives, and parsley to a bowl. Toss to combine.
2. Whisk liquids, and salt in a separate bowl and put over the salad. Mix well and serve. Enjoy!

Nutritional Analysis: 280 calories; 18.6 g fat; 21 g total carbs; 9 g protein

---

Arugula-Zucchini Soup

Cooking Period: 30 minutes

Number of Portions: 4

Required Materials for Recipe:

- 2 tbsp almond butter and olive oil (1 of each)
- Two garlic and 2 leeks
- Four cups zucchini, chopped
- 6 cups vegetable broth
- 10 cups of baby arugula
- Two tablespoons of lemon juice
- Half cup parsley, chopped
- 3-quarter teaspoon salt plus 1-quarter tsp pepper

Instructions for this recipe:

1. Melt some butter and oil together. Cook the garlic and onions for three minutes after adding them to the pan. Bring to a simmer the zucchini, stock, salt, and pepper that you have added to the pot. Cover, and let it cook for 15 mins.
2. After adding the lettuce, let it sit for five minutes. Blend the broth to a smooth consistency. Mix in some cilantro and lemon juice. Serve, and have fun!

Nutritional Analysis: 647 calories; 31.6 g fat; 7 g total carbs; 36 g protein

---

Potato and Parsley Soup

Cooking Period: 40 minutes

Number of Portions: 2

Required Materials for Recipe:

- One onion, sliced
- One tablespoon oil
- One celery stick, diced
- One lb. potatoes, peeled and diced
- 4 cups vegetable stock
- Two tablespoons parsley
- Salt and pepper to taste

Instructions for this recipe:

1. Onions should be added to olive oil that has been heated in a pan. Stirring often, cook for ten mins.
2. The dish would benefit from the addition of celery, potatoes, and half a bunch of parsley.
3. Turn the heat down low, add the stock, and bring it to a boiling. Prepare in 15 minutes.

4. Add the remaining parsley and blend the mixture. Add more stock if required.
5. Season with salt and pepper and reheat. Enjoy!

Nutritional Analysis: 240 calories; 7.2 g fat; 41 g total carbs; 5 g protein

---

Carrot and Parsley Soup

Cooking Period: 22 minutes

Number of Portions: 2

Required Materials for Recipe:

- One bunch of flat-leaf parsley
- 1 oz almond butter
- Two celery stalks, chopped
- One tablespoon of olive oil
- One onion, diced
- One lb. carrots, roughly chopped
- 1 cup almond milk
- Three garlic cloves
- Three ¾ cups of vegetable stock

Instructions for this recipe:

1. Melt some oil and butter in a pan and cook garlic, celery, and onions on low heat for 8 minutes.
2. Increase the heat, add carrots, and cook for just two minutes.
3. Add chicken stock, and cook for 10 minutes after you have reached boiling.
4. Add parsley and cook for 1 minute.
5. Let cool and add the mixture to a blender and blend until smooth.
6. Put on heat and add milk, and stir. Enjoy!

_____

Fig and Arugula Salad

Cooking Period: 15 minutes

Number of Portions: 2

Required Materials for Recipe:

- Three tablespoons of olive oil
- ½ cup walnut halves
- Two teaspoons of balsamic vinegar
- One teaspoon honey
- 5 oz fresh arugula
- ½ cup dried figs, quartered
- One carrot shaved
- 15 oz can unsalted chickpeas, drained and rinsed
- 3 oz goat cheese, crumbled
- 1/8 teaspoon cayenne pepper
- ¾ teaspoon + 1/8 teaspoon salt

Instructions for this recipe:

1. Warm your oven to 375 F.
2. Mix cayenne, walnuts, one tablespoon olive oil, and salt and spread on a baking sheet.
3. Whisk honey, balsamic vinegar, the remaining olive oil, and salt in a little bowl.
4. Toss arugula, chickpeas, carrot, and figs in a separate bowl.
5. Top with toasted walnuts and goat cheese.
6. Add 2 cups of salad to each of the four bowls. Add dressing on top and serve.

Nutritional Analysis: 403 calories; 24 g fat; 35 g total carbs; 13 g protein

Wild rice and Arugula Salad

Cooking Period: 10 minutes

Number of Portions: 2

Required Materials for Recipe:

- ½ teaspoon Dijon mustard
- One tablespoon of olive oil
- ½ teaspoon lemon rind, grated
- One tablespoon lemon juice
- One cup wild rice, cooked
- 1 and a half cups baby arugula, firmly packed
- 1/8 cup red onion
- A pinch of salt, 1 quarter tsp black pepper

Instructions for this recipe:

1. Mix lemon juice, lemon zest, oil, mustard, salt, pepper. Whisk until well combined.
2. Add scallions and wild rice, then mix everything together thoroughly.
3. Add cilantro. Toss, and serve it up.

Nutritional Analysis: 152 calories; 7.7 g fat; 16 g total carbs; 5 g protein

Kale Soup

Cooking Period: 1 hour

Number of Portions: 2

Required Materials for Recipe:

- One yellow onion, chopped
- Two tablespoons of olive oil
- Two tablespoons garlic, chopped
- 8 cups vegetable stock
- One bunch of kale stems was removed, and the leaves chopped
- Six white potatoes, peeled and cubed
- 15 oz can tomato, diced
- Two tablespoons parsley
- One tbsp of Italian seasoning
- Salt - pepper

Instructions for this recipe:

1. Put the olive oil in a stock saucepan. Garlic and onion should be cooked in them until they are tender.
2. After 2 minutes of cooking, add the greens.
3. Stir in the vegetable broth, tomatoes, potatoes, parsley, and Italian seasoning until everything is well combined. Cook broth for twenty-five minutes over a heat setting of the medium. Add little salt and pepper before serving. Serve, and have fun!!

Nutritional Analysis: 277 calories; 4.5 g fat; 51 g total carbs; 9.6 g protein

---

Lemon-Thyme Carrot Soup

Cooking Period: 25 minutes

Number of Portions: 8

Required Materials for Recipe:

- 4 cups carrot slices
- Three tablespoons of lemon juice
- 5 cups vegetable stock
- 1 cup leeks, sliced
- Three teaspoons of dried thyme, crushed
- One bay leaf
- 1/8 teaspoon salt, the same of pepper

Instructions for this recipe:

1. In a saucepan, combine the carrots, onions, and bay leaf. 2. Add the broth. Over medium heat, bring the liquid to a simmer.
2. Stir in some herbs and lemon juice, and season with salt and pepper. Cook for another 5 minutes with the cover on.
3. Take the bay leaf out of the bowl. Use a blender to puree the vegetable combination until it is completely smooth. Heat the pureed concoction that you just returned to the skillet. Serve, and have fun!

Nutritional Analysis: 246 calories; 10.4 g fat; 3 g total carbs; 33 g protein

---

Celery Parsley Soup

Cooking Period: 30 minutes

Number of Portions: 2

Required Materials for Recipe:

- One tablespoon of olive oil
- Two tablespoons of almond butter
- Two leeks
- One of each bunch celery, garlic, potato
- Four handfuls of baby spinach
- ½ bunch of flat-leaf parsley leaves only
- Two tablespoons of lemon juice
- ½ cup vegan yogurt
- One teaspoon of coarse sea salt

Instructions for this recipe:

1. Place the butter in a saucepan and allow it to soften.
2. After a minute, add the potato, leeks, and celery, and continue to simmer for another six minutes, stirring periodically.
3. Sprinkle with salt and garlic, then continue to heat for another two minutes.
4. Pour in four glasses of hot water and bring to a simmer before serving. Change the heat down and continue to simmer for another 10 minutes.
5. Place the chopped parsley and spinach in a blender, then pour the heated broth on top of the mixture. Allow to settle, then process until completely smooth.
6. Blend again after adding the lemon juice and the yogurt.
7. Sprinkle celery stalks on top of the broth, and serve.

Nutritional Analysis: 150 calories; 7 g fat; 19 g total carbs; 4 g protein

---

Kale and Buckwheat Soup

Cooking Period: 30 minutes

Number of Portions: 2

Required Materials for Recipe:

- 1 cup onion
- 1 tbsp vegetable oil
- One teaspoon of garlic, minced
- ¾ cup celery, chopped
- 4 cups vegetable stock
- 1/3 cup buckwheat groats
- 2 cups red rose potato, diced
- One bay leaf
- 2 cups kale, thinly sliced and ribs removed
- One tablespoon of fresh thyme
- Salt - pepper

Instructions for this recipe:

1. Bring a skillet to the temperature of the medium-low fire. Include garlic, onion, and celery in the mix as well. Cook for another 7 minutes with the cover on.
2. Put in water, the stock, the potato, the bay leaf, the cabbage, the buckwheat, and the rosemary. Bring the liquid to a high point to the boil, then cover and continue cooking for another 17 minutes.
3. Add salt and pepper and serve.

Nutritional Analysis: 239 calories; 7 g fat; 30 g total carbs; 15.5 g protein

---

Wild rice and Buckwheat Soup

Cooking Period: 2 hours

Number of Portions: 2

Required Materials for Recipe:

- One onion, grated
- 1 cup brown wild rice
- One tablespoon of olive oil
- Two bay leaves
- One carrot, grated
- ¾ cup raw buckwheat groats
- 4 ½ cup vegetable broth
- Three tablespoons of olive oil
- 9 oz pack of fresh baby spinach

Instructions for this recipe:

1. Soak the wild rice for an hour in a bowl of cool water. Drain, then put it to the side.
2. Bring the oil to a simmer. Add bay leaves and wild rice, and give the mixture a thorough toss.
3. After giving it a stir, add three glasses of vegetable stock and bring to a simmer. Ten minutes should be spent cooking over a medium simmer.
4. Bring the temperature down and add the buckwheat. Wait 25 mins before serving.
5. Pour in the remaining chicken stock. Take the pan off the heat.
6. Add in broccoli. Throw away the bay leaves. Distribute evenly among the six containers.
7. Sprinkle a half teaspoonful of oil into each dish, and then serve.

Nutritional Analysis: 224 calories; 10 g fat; 29 g total carbs; 7.2 g protein

———————————————

Butternut Squash and Turmeric Soup

Cooking Period: 25 minutes

Number of Portions: 4

Required Materials for Recipe:

- 2 and a half lbs. butternut squash
- 2 ½ tablespoons olive oil
- One onion, chopped
- One tablespoon vegetable bouillon base
- Two carrots, chopped
- Two tablespoons of coconut milk
- Two ¼ teaspoons of turmeric
- Two ¼ teaspoons of black pepper

Instructions for this recipe:

1. Create a broth by bringing six glasses of heated water to a simmer, then adding vegetable bouillon base while stirring continuously.
2. Bring a Dutch oven to a high temperature, add the oil, and then sauté the onion for six to eight minutes. Cook for an additional minute after adding the butternut squash and carrots, along with two tablespoons of turmeric and half a teaspoon of black pepper.
3. After lowering the heat to a medium setting, add the stock to the pan and continue to cook the vegetables for another 20 to 22 minutes.
4. Blend the broth until smooth, then stir in the coconut milk and serve.

Nutritional Analysis: 226 calories; 9.2 g fat; 38 g total carbs; 3 g protein

---

Kale Crisps with Paprika Salt

Cooking Period: 30 minutes

Number of Portions: 6

Required Materials for Recipe:

- ½ lb. kale leaves washed thoroughly
- ¼ teaspoon hot smoked paprika
- ½ teaspoon cumin
- One teaspoon of sea salt flakes
- Olive oil

Instructions for this recipe:

1. In your oven reach the temperature of 375 F. Cut stalks from the center of the kale leaves and discard. Chop the leaves into pieces. Completely dry the kale leaves and add to a bowl. Add 1 tbsp of olive oil on top and mix to coat well.
2. Bake for 30 minutes. Mix salt, cumin, and paprika in a bowl and add over the kale. Serve.

Nutritional Analysis: 37 calories; 2.2 g fat; 2.9 g total carbs; 1.5 g protein

---

Nutritional Yeast Pasta

Cooking Period: 15 minutes

Number of Portions: 2

Required Materials for Recipe:

- 8 oz pasta, cooked
- One tablespoon of olive oil
- One teaspoon of all-purpose flour
- 2/3 cup soy milk

- ¼ cup nutritional yeast
- ½ teaspoon mustard
- ½ teaspoon garlic powder
- Salt, to taste

Instructions for this recipe:

1. Place the cooked pasta in a bowl. Warm oil in a saucepan. Incorporate flour and mix well.
2. Slowly pour the soy milk and stir well to combine. Add the nutritional yeast, mustard, garlic, and salt. Mix well to combine.
3. Add the cooked pasta. Stir for about 2 minutes. Enjoy!

Nutritional Analysis: 473 calories; 8 g fat; 85 g total carbs; 14 g protein

---

Agave Glazed Tofu

Cooking Period: 12 minutes

Number of Portions: 2

Required Materials for Recipe:

- One block (12 oz.) of firm tofu, drained
- Three tablespoons of agave syrup
- ¼ cup soy sauce
- Three tablespoons of rice vinegar
- ½ cup canola oil
- One ½-inch ginger, thinly sliced
- ½ teaspoon crushed red pepper flakes

Instructions for this recipe:

1. Drain the excess moisture from the tofu. Slice tofu into nine pieces.
2. Mix agave syrup, soy sauce, vinegar, ginger, and pepper in a little bowl.
3. Add olive oil and heat it. Once heated up, add tofu and cook without stirring for 4 minutes on each side. Remove tofu.
4. Pour the maple mixture into the pan, and cook for just four minutes. Serve and enjoy.

Red rose potato Squash

Cooking Period: 60 minutes

Number of Portions: 4

Required Materials for Recipe:

- One lb. red rose potatoes, peeled, cut
- One butternut squash, peeled, deseeded, sliced
- 14 oz tin tomatoes, chopped
- 10 ½ oz. black rice to serve
- Two tablespoons of vegetable oil
- 14 oz tin coconut milk
- 12 oz. vegetable stock
- One red onion, quartered
- Three red chilies stalks were removed, cut into three
- Two garlic cloves halved
- 2 oz fresh ginger, peeled, thickly sliced

- One teaspoon of each turmeric, coriander, sea salt, just Half tsp cinnamon

Instructions for this recipe:

1. In a food processor, pulse onions, chilies, garlic, ginger, ground coriander, turmeric, cinnamon, and salt until processed.
2. Warm oil in a casserole dish. Incorporate the onion mixture, sauté, and stir correctly for 1 minute.
3. Mix in the vegetable stock, coconut milk, tinned tomatoes, squash, and potato, then bring to a boil. If more flavoring is desired, feel free to add it. Take away from the heat and wait 10 minutes. Enjoy!

Simple Quinoa Fried Rice

Cooking Period: 20 minutes

Number of Portions: 2

Required Materials for Recipe:

- 2 cups quinoa, cooked

- One tablespoon of olive oil
- Two carrots, chopped
- One small head of broccoli, chopped into florets
- One garlic clove, minced
- One teaspoon of pepper
- 1 and a half tbsp soy sauce
- 2 teaspoons of rice wine vinegar, same quantity sesame oil
- One tablespoon onion

Instructions for this recipe:

1. Wash and cook the quinoa in accordance with the directions on the container. Put a saucepan on a burner that is set to medium-high heat. To this, add some olive oil.
2. Give the vegetables three minutes of cooking time. After about three minutes of cooking, add the segments of broccoli and simmer with the garlic.
3. Stir in the pepper, quinoa that has been prepared, soy sauce, and rice wine vinegar. Sauté for about 3 minutes.
4. Add sesame oil. Green scallions, chopped, should be sprinkled on top.
5. Prepare and savor the meal!

Nutritional Analysis: 396 calories; 15 g fat; 55 g total carbs; 17 g protein

---

Peas with Shallots, Mushrooms, and Tarragon

Cooking Period: 20 minutes

Number of Portions: 4

Required Materials for Recipe:

- 14 oz peas, frozen
- Two shallots, sliced
- 2 cups mushrooms, stemmed and sliced

- ¼ cup white wine
- Two tablespoons of olive oil
- One teaspoon of tarragon, chopped
- One teaspoon thyme, chopped
- One tablespoon of lemon zest
- One tablespoon of vegan butter
- Salt and pepper to taste

Instructions for this recipe:

1. Put a skillet on the stove. Include one teaspoon and one tablespoon of olive oil.
2. Place the shallots in the skillet and cook them over medium heat for about three minutes or until they are translucent. Take the pan from the heat, and set it aside.
3. Position the skillet so that it will be heated over medium-high heat.
4. Place the saucepan back over the burner and add the peas and the wine. Bring it up to the boiling point. Take the pan off the heat.
5. Add the scallions and mushrooms and stir to combine. At last, stir in some tarragon, thyme, butter, lemon juice, and seasonings of your choice. Mix together carefully.
6. Serve and appreciate!

Nutritional Analysis: 130 calories; 9.9 g fat; 8 g total carbs; 13 g protein

––––––––––––––––––––

Mango Tempeh Lettuce Wraps

Cooking Period: 20 minutes

Number of Portions: 4

Required Materials for Recipe:

- Eight oz. package tempeh, crumbled

- ¾ cup mango, diced
- ½ cup cucumber, chopped
- ¼ cup roasted cashews, roughly chopped
- ¼ cup mint leaves, chopped
- Eight lettuce leaves
- One tablespoon of grapeseed oil
- Two tablespoons of hoisin sauce
- One tablespoon of lime juice

Instructions for this recipe:

1. Lay a skillet over medium-high heat. Add grape seed oil.
2. Cook tempeh in the skillet for about 3-4 minutes.
3. Add hoisin sauce and lime juice. Remove from the heat and set aside.
4. Place individual lettuce leaves on a working surface.
5. Evenly divide tempeh, chopped mango, cucumber, cashews, and mint leaves.

Nutritional Analysis: 280 calories; 18.4 g fat; 19 g total carbs; 13 g protein

---

Mashed Potatoes with Curried Gravy

Cooking Period: 15 minutes

Number of Portions: 3

Required Materials for Recipe:

- 13 oz coconut milk
- 2 lbs. red potatoes, peeled and chopped
- 1/3 cup tomato sauce
- One onion, chopped
- Two tablespoons of olive oil

- 1 teaspoon of each ingredients (cumin seeds, mustard seeds, fenugreek powder)
- One tablespoon of coriander
- Two tsp of turmeric

Instructions for this recipe:

1. Bring a saucepan of water and some large potatoes to a boil, and cook the potatoes until they are fork-tender about 15 to 20 minutes. After draining off the surplus water, put it to the side.
2. Saute the shallots with the salt in a large saucepan for about three to four minutes.
3. After cooking for an additional one to two minutes, add the cumin, mustard seeds, half a teaspoonful of coriander, and one teaspoon of turmeric to the saucepan. Take the pan off the heat.
4. Place the mashed potatoes that have been boiled in a dish and add the onion combination that has been spiced. Combine the two ingredients thoroughly.
5. In a small saucepan, mix the coconut milk along with one teaspoon each of fenugreek, turmeric, and coriander to a simmer. To flavor, add salt, and combine everything thoroughly.
6. Pour the sauce over the potatoes that have been pureed. Enjoy!

Nutritional Analysis: 824 calories; 45 g fat; 62 g carbs; 13 g protein

---

Mushroom Stroganoff

Cooking Period: 15 minutes

Number of Portions: 4

Required Materials for Recipe:

- One lb. button mushrooms, sliced (substitution for beef)
- 9 oz pasta of choice
- One onion, chopped
- Four garlic cloves minced
- 1 cup vegetable broth
- Two tablespoons of almond butter plus One cup Almond Milk
- 1-quarter cup flour
- One teaspoon (each) thyme, salt, and 1/4 tsp pepper

Instructions for this recipe:

1. Pasta should be prepared under package directions. Drain.
2. Compose a sauce by combining broth, milk, flour, thyme, salt, and pepper. In a pan, melt butter.
3. Put in the garlic and onion and let them cook for 5 minutes. Mushrooms should be added and cooked for a further 5 minutes.
4. Cook for 4 to 5 minutes after adding the broth mixture. Toss the spaghetti with the sauce and combine thoroughly. Heat for a minute or two, then serve.

Nutritional Analysis: 515 calories; 32 g fat; 65 g total carbs; 16 g protein

---

French Stewed Vegetable (Ratatouille)

Cooking Period: 60 minutes

Number of Portions: 4

Required Materials for Recipe:

- Four large tomatoes, peeled, seeded, and chopped
- Four small zucchinis, sliced

- Two eggplants, quartered lengthwise, sliced
- A small bunch of basil, torn
- Four tablespoons of olive oil
- Two onions, chopped
- Two red peppers, seeded, chopped
- Two garlic cloves crushed
- ½ teaspoon sugar
- Pepper - salt

Instructions for this recipe:

1. Saute onions in oil for ten minutes, rotating them frequently. Increase the heat, stir in the zucchini and eggplant, and continue to sauté for another three minutes.
2. To the bowl, add the minced garlic, crushed red pepper, sugar, powdered black pepper, and half of the cilantro.
3. Stir in the vegetables, then continue to simmer for another ten minutes. Serve immediately with the remaining cilantro sprinkled on top. Enjoy!

Sautéed Cabbage

Cooking Period: 20 minutes

Number of Portions: 6

Required Materials for Recipe:

- 3 lbs. green cabbage, cored, shredded
- Two tablespoons of olive oil

- 1 ½ teaspoons cumin seeds
- 1 ½ teaspoons turmeric
- 1 ½ teaspoons kosher salt

Instructions for this recipe:

1. Sauté cumin seeds in olive oil, for 30 seconds.
2. Mix in the cabbage, turmeric, and salt and cook for 20mins. Enjoy.

Roasted Cauliflower and Tempeh

Cooking Period: 45 minutes

Number of Portions: 4

Required Materials for Recipe:

- Two tablespoons of avocado oil
- 3 cups cauliflower florets
- 8 oz tempeh, cut into cubes
- Half teaspoon turmeric, grounded
- 1 quarter tsp salt
- One tbsp water
- Two teaspoons of miso paste
- One green leaf lettuce, trimmed and cleaned
- 1 batch of vegan shiitake bacon

Instructions for this recipe:

1. Warm your oven at 350 F.
2. Put oil over the cauliflower, add tempeh, turmeric, and salt and toss to mix. Spread this onto a baking sheet and bake for 26 minutes.

3. Mix water and miso in a bowl, transfer the roasted tempeh and cauliflower to it, and toss.
4. Divide lettuce among four plates. Top with shiitake bacon and walnuts. Add the tempeh and cauliflower, drizzle with dressing and serve.

Nutritional Analysis: 322 calories; 22 g fat; 19 g total carbs; 22 g protein

---

Ratatouille Quinoa Stew

Cooking Period: 30 minutes

Number of Portions: 10

Required Materials for Recipe:

- 1 ½ cups eggplant, diced
- 1 ½ cups zucchini squash, quartered and sliced
- Two garlic cloves minced
- 1 ½ cups onion, chopped
- ½ cup quinoa
- 6 cups vegetable stock
- 3 cups crushed tomatoes
- ¼ cup jarred hot peppers, chopped
- Three bay leaves
- One tablespoon of olive oil
- 1 ½ teaspoon dry thyme leaves

Instructions for this recipe:

1. Bring a Dutch oven to a temperature of medium heat. Mix in the zucchini, shallots, and garlic in addition to the eggplant. Prepare for approximately 2 minutes.
2. Add quinoa, bay leaves, and thyme, and sauté for about 8 minutes more.

3. Add vegetable broth, tomatoes, and chilies. Bring it up to the boiling point.
4. Place a cover on the pan and lower the heat. Cook it for an additional twenty minutes after that. Take the pan off the heat.
5. Prepare and savor the meal!

Nutritional Analysis: 90 calories; 2 g fat; 16 g total carbs; 9 g protein

---

Lemon Vegetable Quinoa

Cooking Period: 30 minutes

Number of Portions: 6

Required Materials for Recipe:

- One and ½ cups quinoa
- 3 mugs water
- One cup of each onion, carrots, sweet pepper
- 2 cups zucchini, diced
- 1/3 cup fresh basil, chopped
- One tablespoon of olive oil
- One tablespoon of garlic, minced
- 1 ½ teaspoons smoked paprika
- Two teaspoons of dried oregano

- Two teaspoons of dried thyme
- One tablespoon of lemon juice
- Salt - pepper

Instructions for this recipe:

1. Begin by bringing the water to a simmer. After adding fresh quinoa, reduce the heat to a medium setting, cover, and let the mixture simmer for about 15 minutes.
2. While that is going on, put some olive oil in a saucepan and cook it over medium heat.
3. Cook the onion and garlic for about seven minutes, stirring occasionally. After adding the oregano, thyme, and paprika, continue to heat until the mixture becomes aromatic.
4. After an additional three minutes of cooking, add the vegetables. The peppers and zucchini should be added after that, and the cooking time should be approximately 8 minutes with frequent stirring. Take the pan off the heat.
5. Mix the quinoa that has been prepared with a light hand in the saucepan. To finish, season with salt, pepper, lemon juice, and basil leaves. Combine thoroughly.
6. Serve while it is still steaming, and have fun with it!

Nutritional Analysis: 201 calories; 5 g fat; 33 g total carbs; 17 g protein

---

Wild rice Tabbouleh

Cooking Period: 30 minutes

Number of Portions: 4

Required Materials for Recipe:

- 7 oz cherry tomatoes, halved
- 7 oz puy wild rice, rinsed and drained

- One bunch of spring onions, chopped
- One bunch of parsley, chopped
- One bunch of fresh mint, chopped
- One lemon, juiced
- Extra virgin olive oil

Instructions for this recipe:

1. Bring the water with some salt to a boil, add the wild rice, and cook until tender. Drain and set aside to cool.
2. Mix the wild rice, onions, tomatoes, parsley, and mint in a bowl. Drizzle with oil and fresh lemon juice, and toss to combine. Serve.

Nutritional Analysis: 175 calories; 4.9 g fat; 21 g total carbs; 16 g protein

---

Red rose potato Tofu Curry

Cooking Period: 30 minutes

Number of Portions: 4

Required Materials for Recipe:

- 1/3 cup green beans, cut lengthwise
- 14 oz tofu, cubed
- One red rose potato, peeled and cubed
- One onion, chopped
- One yellow pepper, cubed
- One red pepper, cubed
- 1 cup coconut milk
- ½ cup water
- Two tablespoons of coconut oil
- Six green chilies grind into a paste

- Two strands of curry leaves
- Two tablespoons turmeric
- One tablespoon of ginger and garlic paste
- ½ teaspoon cumin, ground
- Salt, to taste

Instructions for this recipe:

1. Put a saucepan on the stove and turn the heat. After adding the oil and chile paste, continue to heat the mixture while frequently swirling it until it has browned.
2. Stir the onion, ginger, and garlic puree into the mixture while it is still warm. Cook for a few more minutes after adding the cumin and turmeric.
3. After a few more minutes of cooking, add the potato pieces from the red rose potato.
4. After adding green beans and green bell peppers, continue to prepare the vegetables until they have a caramelized appearance.
5. Stir in some tofu, some water, some chili leaves, and some coconut milk.
6. Take the pan off the flame. Accompany the dish with prepared rice.

Nutritional Analysis: 412 calories; 29.3 g fat; 24 g carbs; 21 g protein

---

Chili Garlic Tofu with Sesame Broccolini

Cooking Period: 25 minutes

Number of Portions: 4

Required Materials for Recipe:

- 12 oz tofu, chopped

- ½ teaspoon cracked peppercorns, fresh
- Four garlic cloves, shredded
- 8 oz broccolini
- Two tablespoons of coconut oil
- Salt, to taste
- One tablespoon of chili garlic sauce
- Two tablespoons honey
- One 1/2 teaspoons soy sauce
- Two small roasted and sliced seaweed sheets
- One tablespoon of toasted sesame seeds to garnish

Instructions for this recipe:

1. After draining the tofu, wipe it with a cloth and set it aside. Repeat the drying process, then chop the meat into minute pieces.
2. Place the saucepan over a heat setting medium and add the oil. Cook the garlic, salt, and pepper together until the garlic becomes aromatic.
3. Add in the tofu and heat for approximately 5–6 minutes or until it has a light golden color.
4. Pour some water into the saucepan, then position it on the stove. After the water has come to a simmer, place the steamer container in the pot, and then add the broccolini. Steamed for a total of six minutes.
5. In a separate dish, combine the honey, soy sauce, and chili sauce, then put it aside.
6. Take the garlic out of the pan and set it aside. Add the broccolini to the pan, and make sure it is evenly coated by swirling it around. After toasting the sesame seeds, add them to the dish and combine them for at least a minute. To serve, divide the tofu between two dishes and drizzle the chile sauce on top of it.
7. Finish with a layer of seaweed.

Nutritional Analysis: 351 calories; 25.7 g fat; 21 g carbs; 16 g protein

Red rose potato Wild rice Dal

Cooking Period: 10 minutes

Number of Portions: 2

Required Materials for Recipe:

- 1 cup red wild rice
- Four garlic cloves
- One red rose potato, diced
- 3 cups water
- Two tablespoons of olive oil
- One teaspoon of cumin seeds
- One tablespoon of garam masala spice
- One teaspoon of fenugreek leaves
- One teaspoon honey
- Two bay leaves
- 1 serrano chili pepper
- One yellow onion, diced
- One tablespoon of fresh ginger, shredded
- Two tomatoes, diced
- Salt, to taste
- One handful of baby fresh cilantro leaves or chopped scallions for garnish.
- Three tablespoons of ghee or coconut oil
- One teaspoon of each seed (cumin, black mustard, fennel)
- Eight curry leaves

Instructions for this recipe:

1. Put the wild rice in a dish and pour enough water to submerge it.

2. Bring the oil to a simmer in a saucepan. After the shallots have been sautéed for at least three minutes, ginger should be added. Garlic, seasonings, bay leaves, chiles, and salt should all be added now. Toasted seasonings should be given a full minute of swirling throughout the process. Honey should be used to flavor the red rose potatoes.
3. Wild rice, after having been drained, can be added to a stew along with tinned vegetables and water after the rice has been drained. As soon as everything reaches a simmer, place the lid on the saucepan. Maintain on for 15 to 17 minutes.
4. Get ready to heat the oil for seasoning. In the saucepan, adds the oil or butter of your choice to it. Curry leaves, and seeds should be combined and then added. Stir the mixture for approximately 40 to 45 seconds or until you hear a crackling sound. Remove the pot from the fire.
5. Garnish each serving with some shredded coconut and chopped cilantro. Enjoy!

Nutritional Analysis: 721 calories; 37.8 g fat; 76 g carbs; 26 g protein

---

Grilled Cauliflower Steaks

Cooking Period: 20 minutes

Number of Portions: 4

Required Materials for Recipe:

- One cauliflower head
- Six tablespoons of vegetable oil
- Two tablespoons of fresh lime juice
- One bunch of scallions, trimmed

- One piece of ginger
- One garlic clove
- ½ cup cilantro leaves
- Salt - pepper

Instructions for this recipe:

1. Place the cauliflower with the core side down on a plain surface. Starting at the cauliflower's center line, slice from top to bottom into 4 ½" 'steaks' (save the florets that break up).
2. Drizzle cauliflower steaks, scallions, and florets with four tablespoons of oil.
3. Grill the scallions for 2 minutes over medium-high heat, then grill the steaks for 8-10 minutes per side. Finally, grill any loose florets for 5-7 minutes.
4. Mix ginger, garlic, cilantro, lime juice, and the remaining oil in a blender and blend to make the sauce. Use water to thin if needed.
5. Serve the cauliflower steaks and scallions with cilantro sauce.

Nutritional Analysis: 92 calories; 9.2 g fat; 1.6 g total carbs; 1.3 g protein

---

Sweet Korean Wild Rice

Cooking Period: 20 minutes

Number of Portions: 4

Required Materials for Recipe:

For the sauce:

- 2 cups water
- Three tbsp of agave syrup

- Two garlic cloves minced
- One small ginger, minced
- One teaspoon of sesame oil
- 1-quarter cup soy sauce
- Just Half teaspoon red pepper flakes

For the Wild rice:

- Two green onions, chopped
- One tablespoon oil
- One tablespoon of sesame seeds
- 1/2 yellow onion, chopped
- 1 cup red wild rice

Instructions for this recipe:

1. Put all of the specified ingredients into a small dish and mix them together.
2. Some oil should be added to a frying pan and warm it. Sauté the onion until it has lost its crunch and turned a light golden color. Along with the wild rice, pour the marinade into the bowl.
3. Place the lid on the pot and place it over low heat. Continue to prepare the wild rice in this manner until it is delicate and fully cooked, which should take about 7 to 10 minutes.
4. Top with some toasted sesame seeds and chopped green scallion. Enjoy!

Nutritional Analysis: 336 calories; 11 g fat; 48 g total carbs; 14 g protein

---

Cauliflower Fried Rice

Cooking Period: 30 minutes

Number of Portions: 4

Required Materials for Recipe:

- One lb. tofu
- 1/2 cup peas, fresh or frozen
- One tablespoon of ginger, minced
- Three garlic, 1 quarter cup onions
- One cauliflower head, riced
- Two carrots
- Two tablespoons oil
- Three tablespoons of soy sauce

Instructions for this recipe:

1. Press the tofu and allow it to settle. After that, do so in a dish by slightly crumbling it. Set aside.
2. Pour some oil into a skillet and set it over a heat setting that is somewhere in the middle. After about a minute, add the garlic and ginger, and continue to sauté until the garlic and ginger are faintly browned and fragrant. After adding the tofu and stirring it for approximately six minutes, the tofu should be browned and fully prepared. Put the tofu in a separate bowl.
3. In a saucepan, add a little bit more olive oil and then stir in the vegetables. Sauté for about 2-3 minutes until tender.
4. Include the peas in the rice made from cauliflower and toss them in until they are incorporated. Prepare the cauliflower for about 6 to 8 minutes in the oven until it is cooked. Include the prepared tofu and green scallions in the dish.
5. Distribute the cooked rice made with cauliflower. Enjoy!

Nutritional Analysis: 437 calories; 32.2 g fat; 22 g total carbs; 22 g protein

---

Potato and Pepper Bake

Cooking Period: 1 hour

Number of Portions: 4

Required Materials for Recipe:

- 4 lbs. potatoes, peeled, cubed
- One lb. roasted peppers in oil
- Two tablespoons of coriander seeds
- One tablespoon of olive oil
- Salt - pepper

Instructions for this recipe:

1. Warm your oven to 375 F.
2. Add the potatoes to a tin, together with oil, salt, and pepper.
3. Peppers can be sliced thinly and laid out in a row on top of the potatoes. Toss in some coriander seeds for flavor.
4. Bake for at least 60 mins. Potatoes are tender, golden brown, and beginning to crisp up around the edges.
5. Once the potatoes are prepared, take them out of the oven and place them in a serving dish. Serve.

Nutritional Analysis: 436 calories; 4.5 g fat; 92 g total carbs; 12 g protein

---

Wild rice and Cherry Tomatoes

Cooking Period: 25 minutes

Number of Portions: 2

Required Materials for Recipe:

- 3 ½ oz red wild rice
- Eight cherry tomatoes halved
- One teaspoon of vegetable oil
- One red onion, chopped
- ½ teaspoon curry powder
- ½ red chili, deseeded, chopped
- One tablespoon of fresh ginger, peeled, chopped

- One garlic clove, chopped
- ½ handful of baby spinach
- ½ cup vegetable stock
- Salt and pepper to taste
- One tablespoon coriander, chopped, to garnish

Instructions for this recipe:

1. Put a little bit of oil in a saucepan. Add some ginger, onion, garlic, and chili to the skillet.
2. After approximately four minutes of cooking time, add the curry powder, wild rice, and cherry tomatoes to the pan. Continue to cook for another two minutes.
3. Pour in the chicken stock. The cooking time for wild rice can range anywhere from 17 to 20 minutes, so reduce the temperature and let it simmer.
4. Wilt the green spinach by cooking it in a pan with a little amount of water while stirring it periodically until it is wilted.
5. Sprinkle some coriander on top, and serve.

Nutritional Analysis: 705 calories; 38.1 g fat; 40 g total carbs; 13 g protein

---

Mushrooms Red rose potatoes Patties

Cooking Period: 50 minutes

Number of Portions: 4

Required Materials for Recipe:

- Three red rose potatoes, chopped
- Ten white button mushrooms, chopped
- 2 cups water
- One onion, chopped
- Three garlic
- Three tablespoons of Italian Herbs
- One tablespoon of olive oil

- Salt and pepper to taste

Instructions for this recipe:

1. Inside a pot add water and sweet potatoes, and bring the water to a boil until the red rose potatoes are soft and tender.
2. Remove from heat and drain excess water. Mash the red rose potatoes.
3. In a small, preheat the oil, garlic, onion, and mushrooms and cook until soft.
4. Add some Italian herbs, salt, and pepper. Roll and shape the mixture into patties.

5. Lay the patties onto a baking sheet. Bake the cakes for about 15mins. Serve.

Nutritional Analysis: 249 calories; 5.2 g fat; 48.2 g carbs; 4.8 g protein

---

Mushroom Quinoa Patties

Cooking Period: 20 minutes

Number of Portions: 3

Required Materials for Recipe:

- 1 cup mushrooms, chopped
- ½ cup quinoa, cooked
- Four tablespoons spelled flour
- Two red onions, sliced
- Two tablespoons of grapeseed oil

- Salt - pepper

Instructions for this recipe:

1. In a food processor, combine the mushrooms, quinoa, and red onions along with the salt and pepper. Pulse the combination until it is completely homogeneous.
2. Place the combination in a dish, and then transform the mixture into patties using your hands. Spelled flour should be used to coat the burgers.
3. Melt some oil in a cast-iron saucepan that has been preheated to a medium temperature. After adding the burgers, roast them for eight minutes on each side. Take the pan off the heat. Enjoy!

Nutritional Analysis: 199 calories; 5.1 g fat; 33.1 g carbs; 6.9 g protein

---

Vegan Ground Beef

Cooking Period: 10 minutes

Number of Portions: 4

Required Materials for Recipe:

- One head of cauliflower, cut into florets, shredded
- 8 oz Portobello mushrooms, shredded (substitution for beef)

- One onion, chopped
- Two carrots, shredded
- 1 cup raw pumpkin seeds
- ¼ cup sun-dried tomatoes, chopped

- Two garlic cloves minced

Instructions for this recipe:

1. Add pumpkin seeds and sun-dried tomatoes to a blender and pulse until smooth. Transfer to a bowl.
2. Cook mushrooms, cauliflower, onion, carrots, and garlic in a skillet for about 6-8 minutes.

3. Add tomato paste and Serve.

Nutritional Analysis: 388 calories; 15.4 g fat; 58 g total carbs; 17 g protein

---

Smoothie Bowl with Cauliflower and Greens

Cooking Period: 5 minutes

Number of Portions: 4

Required Materials for Recipe:

- Half cup cauliflower
- The same proportion of One cup spinach, blueberries, milk (almond)
- 2 Tbsp of almond butter
- Three tablespoons of hemp hearts
- 1/2 cup zucchini
- One teaspoon of ground cinnamon

- toppings of your choice

Instructions for this recipe:

1. Place all of the ingredients on the list in a blender and process until the mixture has a smooth buttery texture.
2. Lay the garnishes of your choosing on top, and then serve.

Nutritional Analysis: 153 calories; 8.1 g fat; 19 g total carbs; 3 g protein

---

Desserts/Snacks
Strawberry Coconut Chia Pudding

Cooking Period: 15 minutes

Number of Portions: 3

Required Materials for Recipe:

- Three Tbsp chia seeds
- One tsp of vanilla extract
- Just 1 cup almond milk, One can coconut milk
- toppings of your choice

For the strawberry jam:

- 1 cup strawberries

- One teaspoon of coconut sugar

Instructions for this recipe:

1. Combine together chia, milk, and vanilla, and refrigerate overnight.
2. Put strawberries and coconut sugar into a pan and cook for just 15 minutes.
3. Once cooked, blend the jam till smooth.
4. Add coconut milk or cream and mix well. Add one layer of strawberry jam to the bottom of the glass jars. Add chia pudding and coconut milk on top.

5. Add more jam and berries. Serve and enjoy!

Nutritional Analysis: 74 calories; 2.8 g fat; 9 g total carbs; 3 g protein

Mango Chia Seed Pudding

Cooking Period: 60 minutes

Number of Portions: 4

Required Materials for Recipe:

- Two cups coconut milk
- Only 1/2 cup chia seeds
- Two mangoes, sliced
- Three tablespoons of coconut nectar
- One teaspoon of vanilla extract
- 1/4 teaspoon cardamom

Instructions for this recipe:

1. Add chia seeds, cardamom, vanilla, coconut milk, and coconut nectar to a mason jar. Mix until well combined and refrigerate for 1 hour.
2. Add sliced mango to the blender and blend into a puree

3. Add puree to the mason jar and serve.

Nutritional Analysis: 254 calories; 9.3 g fat; 38 g total carbs; 8 g protein

---

Butternut Squash Pudding

Cooking Period: 40 minutes

Number of Portions: 3 to 5

Required Materials for Recipe:

- One butternut squash, cut in half lengthwise
- Four tablespoons of coconut milk
- 1/2 teaspoon cinnamon

- One banana
- Only 1/2 cup dates

Instructions for this recipe:

1. Place butternut squash on a tin and cut side down.
2. Bake in a warm oven (at 350 F) for about 40 minutes.
3. After 40 minutes, scrape the pulp with a spoon and add it to a blender along with the remaining ingredients.
4. Blend until smooth, and serve!

Nutritional Analysis: 83 calories; 0.6g fat; 20g total carbs; 1g protein

---

Spiced Applesauce

Cooking Period: 25 minutes

Number of Portions: 6-8

Required Materials for Recipe:

- 1 oz. apple cider vinegar
- ½ cup sugar, plain or toasted
- One cinnamon stick
- 4 lbs. mixed apples, cored, chopped
- 1/2 teaspoon salt
- One orange peel strip
- 1/4 teaspoon rose water

Instructions for this recipe:

1. Remove the core from the apples and then slice them into small chunks. After placing the chopped apples, apple cider vinegar, citrus zest, sugar, a cinnamon stick, and salt in a Dutch oven together, give everything a good stir until it is thoroughly combined. After 15 minutes, the apples should be wilted and bubbling in their own liquids, so make sure the cover is on tight.

2.   Continue to cook, maintaining a low flame for another ten minutes, stirring the mixture frequently, until the apples are fork-tender. After the sauce has finished cooking, take out the cinnamon stick and the orange rind, and then puree it in a blender until it is completely smooth. To achieve the desired consistency, add additional apple juice.

3. Place the apple sauce in the glass vessels, and before serving, chill them in the refrigerator.

Nutritional Analysis: 92 calories; 9.2 g fat; 1.6 g total carbs; 1.3 g protein

---

Coconut Cream Shake

Cooking Period: 5 minutes

Number of Portions: 2

Required Materials for Recipe:

- Two teaspoons matcha
- One large banana, frozen
- One cup coconut milk
- ¼ cup ice cubes

Instructions for this recipe:

1. Add all the cream shake ingredients to a blender. Blitz and obtain a mixture creamy and smooth.

2. Put into chilled glasses and serve with your desired toppings. Enjoy!

Nutritional Analysis: 110 calories; 6.1 g fat; 10 g total carbs; 4 g protein

---

Cucumber Detox Smoothie

Cooking Period: 5 minutes

Number of Portions: 2

Required Materials for Recipe:

- 3-4-inch chunk cucumber
- 1 cup water, more if desired
- 2 mugs mixed berries
- Just 1 cup almond milk
- One banana
- One tbsp of chia seeds
- One apple, cored
- 1 cup kale
- One lemon, juiced
- ½ cup Italian flat-leaf parsley

Instructions for this recipe:

1. Add all the fresh smoothie ingredients to a high-speed blender.
2. Blitz to combine until smooth.
3. Add more water if needed.
4. Pour into a chilled glass and serve.

Nutritional Analysis: 410 calories; 11.3 g fat; 70 g total carbs; 12 g protein

_____

Almond Avocado Matcha

Cooking Period: 5 minutes

Number of Portions: 2

Required Materials for Recipe:

- One teaspoon matcha
- 1 cup ice
- 1.5 oz. red lettuce
- 1 cup vanilla almond milk
- One pear, chopped
- One tablespoon of almond butter
- 1/2 avocado, pitted

Instructions for this recipe:

1. Add all the fresh smoothie ingredients to a high-speed blender.
2. Blitz to combine until smooth.

3. Pour into a chilled glass and serve.

Nutritional Analysis: 313 calories; 16.7 g fat; 38 g total carbs; 6 g protein

Golden Flax Seed Pudding

Cooking Period: 50 minutes

Number of Portions: 1

Required Materials for Recipe:

- One teaspoon agave
- ¾ cup almond milk
- ¾ teaspoon golden milk spice mix
- Two tablespoons of coconut yogurt
- Three tablespoons of golden flax seeds
- ¾ cup fruits

Instructions for this recipe:

1. Make golden milk according to package instructions. Mix golden flax seeds with golden milk and soak for 1 hour, stirring often. Mix with two tablespoons of coconut yogurt. Add agave.
2. Add golden flax pudding to a bowl and top with the fruits and/or edible flowers. Serve.

Nutritional Analysis: 387 calories; 16.1 g fat; 59 g total carbs; 8 g protein

---

Golden Turmeric Crackers

Cooking Period: 25 minutes

Number of Portions: 1 bowl

Required Materials for Recipe:

- ½ teaspoon baking powder
- One and a 1/3 cups almond flour
- ½ teaspoon turmeric powder
- One teaspoon of olive oil
- ½ cup water
- ½ teaspoon salt

Instructions for this recipe:

1. Warm your oven (400° F).
2. Incorporate dry ingredients to a bowl, whisk well, and slowly add water and olive oil. Mix and knead with your hands. Add more flour or water if needed.
3. Roll out the fresh dough on lightly floured parchment paper. Cut the dough with a pizza cutter into rectangles diagonally to create triangles. Put the parchment paper onto a baking sheet.
4. Bake for 20 minutes. Serve.

Nutritional Analysis: 647 calories; 5 g fat; 128 g total carbs; 17 g protein

---

Crispy Edamame

Cooking Period: 30 minutes

Number of Portions: 4

Required Materials for Recipe:

- Two teaspoons of olive oil
- 4 cups edamame, frozen and shelled
- ½ teaspoon salt
- ¼ teaspoon black pepper

Instructions for this recipe:

1. Thaw edamame for 1 hour. Place on a dish towel and dry.
2. Preheat the oven to 350 F. Add edamame to the tin and drizzle with olive oil. Season with salt and pepper.
3. Bake for 30-35 mins. stirring every 8-10 minutes. Serve.

Nutritional Analysis: 209 calories; 10.3 g fat; 15 g total carbs; 17 g protein

---

Dried Strawberries

Cooking Period: 3 hours 15 minutes

Number of Portions: 3

Required Materials for Recipe:

- One lb. strawberries washed and dried

Instructions for this recipe:

1. Cut the strawberries into wedges. Lay the strawberries in a baking dish that will not stick.
2. Cook for a total of two hours in a warm oven (300°F). Remove the strawberry wedges from the pan and then turn them over. Cook for another 30 minutes.
3. Remove the strawberries from the oven and let them rest for a while. Serve

Nutritional Analysis: 48 calories; 0 g fat; 11.5 g total carbs; 1 g protein

CONCLUSION

You should strive for a well-rounded diet. Whole grains and at least five servings of fresh fruits and vegetables are part of this. There's also evidence that regularly eating nuts, such as peanuts or cashews, can help reduce your risk of developing gallstones.

Printed in Great Britain
by Amazon

38640394R00071